## ON THE
# FIELD WITH...
## MEGAN RAPINOE,
## ALEX MORGAN,
## CARLI LLOYD, and
## MALLORY PUGH

ON THE
# FIELD WITH...
# MEGAN RAPINOE, ALEX MORGAN, CARLI LLOYD, and MALLORY PUGH

## MATT CHRISTOPHER®

**The #1 Sports Series for Kids**

**Text by Stephanie Peters**

LITTLE, BROWN AND COMPANY
New York   Boston

Little, Brown and Company
Hachette Book Group
1290 Avenue of the Americas, New York, NY 10104
Visit us at LBYR.com
mattchristopher.com

First Edition: January 2020

Little, Brown and Company is a division of Hachette Book Group, Inc. The
Little, Brown name and logo are trademarks of Hachette Book Group, Inc.

The publisher is not responsible for websites (or their content) that are not owned
by the publisher.

Matt Christopher® is a registered trademark of Matt Christopher Royalties, Inc.

Text written by Stephanie Peters

Library of Congress Control Number: 2019952178

ISBNs: 978-0-316-49787-9 (pbk.), 978-0-316-49785-5 (ebook)

Printed in the United States of America

LSC-C

10 9 8 7 6 5 4 3 2 1

# CONTENTS

# MALLORY PUGH

# MEGAN RAPINOE

# CARLI LLOYD

Morgan Brian and Alex Morgan celebrate with Carli Lloyd after she scores her second goal against Japan during the 2015 Women's World Cup, in Vancouver.

Carli Lloyd with the ball during a friendly match against Mexico leading up to the 2019 Women's World Cup. Team USA won 3–0.

# CHAPTER 1
# 1982–2003

## THE KICK SEEN ROUND THE WORLD

*Let me just bomb this from the mid stripe. What the heck...*

That was the thought that crossed Carli Lloyd's mind a split second before she launched the most famous kick in the history of women's soccer. As the ball sailed half the length of the field, more than fifty thousand fans leaped to their feet in Vancouver's BC Place Stadium. Millions more watching at home held their breath.

On the field, Carli and the rest of Team USA followed the ball with their eyes, their bodies, and their hearts. "It felt like an eternity watching the ball soar through the air," Carli recalled. "I saw the keeper [Japan's Ayumi Kaihori] backing up, and I was like, *No!* And then I saw her reaching back, and I was like, *No!* I saw it brush her fingertips."

Everyone agonized with her. And then—

"Off the post and *in*!" a television announcer screamed.

"This is absolutely world-class," a second announcer enthused.

Back home, friends and fans jumped for joy, hugged, and shouted with amazement. The deafening roar inside the stadium grew even louder as Carli raced across the field, arms raised in celebration and a mile-wide grin on her face, to fling herself into the crushing embrace of her teammates.

That amazing goal all but sealed the victory for the United States Women's National Team (USWNT) over Japan in the 2015 Women's World Cup finals. Unbelievably, it wasn't Carli's first goal of the game. It wasn't even her second. That long bomb was her third. Even more astounding, she scored the hat trick in just sixteen minutes! No player, male or female, had *ever* racked up that many goals in so short a period in any World Cup final game.

"It was the greatest individual performance in a World Cup final ever," one sports journalist reported the next day. "End of discussion."

Lloyd made that third goal look almost effortless. But those who have followed her career know that the road to that moment was anything but smooth.

Rewind her timeline twelve years, and you'll see a very different Carli Lloyd. Not the powerful athlete who unleashed a blast that catapulted her into soccer history, but a tearful twenty-one-year-old on the brink of leaving the sport forever.

Dial back even further, though, and you'll find a young girl who couldn't wait to lace up her cleats and hit the field.

Carli Lloyd was born on July 16, 1982, the oldest of three children in the Lloyd family. Her parents, Stephen and Pamela, worked hard to provide a good home in Delran, New Jersey, a small town about twenty minutes outside Philadelphia, for Carli, Stephen Junior, and Ashley. From a very early age, Carli was an athletic tomboy who preferred mowing the lawn to playing dress-up and baseball cards to Barbie dolls. "You [would] never find a ribbon or a bow on me," she said of her childhood self.

Carli started playing soccer when she was five years old. Her father helped coach her team, the Delran Dynamite. Her other coach, Karen Thorton, got the most out of players with her positivity and sense of fun. Together, the two coaches encouraged Carli and her teammates to enjoy the sport, not live and breathe it.

That came later for Carli.

Even at that young age, Carli stood out as a star with natural talent. She absorbed coaching the way a sponge absorbs water. If the Dynamite fell behind, she did whatever she could to get them back in the game. Sometimes, that meant taking charge of the ball—which is exactly what she did during one game when she was eleven.

The Dynamite was down a goal when Carli collected the ball from her keeper. Knowing they needed to score, she took off, dribbling around one defender, finding a gap between two others, and charging down the length of the field until she was within scoring range of the opponent's goal. Then— *pow!* She unleashed a kick. The ball rocketed past the keeper and—*swish!*—billowed the strings of the net.

Whether the game ended in a win, loss, or tie, Carli doesn't recall. Three things did stick with her, however. One, she had just made a really big play; two, she liked making big plays; and three, she might not have made that big play if she hadn't put in extra practice on her own.

Whenever she had free time at home, day or night, Carli took a ball to the street outside her house. There, she practiced her footwork and ball control with her favorite partner: a particular stretch of Black Baron Drive's curb. The curb was long, but it was no more than a few inches high. Kick the ball too high, and she'd have to chase it into a neighbor's yard. Hit it too hard, and the rebound might be too tough to control. Find that sweet spot, though, and she could play against the curb for hours.

And she did—by her own estimate, she bounced her ball against that curb for close to two thousand passes a day, every day, for nearly ten years!

Carli also spent hours playing pickup games with whoever happened to be playing at the neighborhood soccer field. Being her own boss on the field gave her new insights into how the game could be played. With the freedom to think for herself, she learned to "read" the field, anticipate how the action might unfold, and improvise creative ways to make the most of passing, scoring, and other offensive opportunities.

By the time she was twelve, Carli's skill level had outgrown what the town league could offer. So as much as she loved playing for the Dynamite, she decided to try out for a more competitive team, the South Jersey Select.

The Select was one of the area's top-tier squads. The tryouts drew crowds of girls from across the region. All were vying for just a handful of spots. Carli worked hard to impress the evaluators with her ball-handling ability and overall athleticism. But she feared what she showed them wasn't enough.

It wasn't. She got cut.

Not seeing her name on the roster was "a colossal, crush-my-world setback," Carli said. Her interest in soccer had grown leaps and bounds since she'd first started playing. She was even beginning to daydream about a career playing her favorite sport. Being told she wasn't good enough was a devastating blow.

Yet it might have been the best thing that could have happened to her.

Denied a slot on the Select, she found her way onto a different team for players under the age of thirteen, the Medford Strikers club. It was a match made in heaven, with a coach, Joe Dadura, who was as nurturing as he was competitive, supportive parents who traveled with their daughters to distant tournaments, and best of all, friendly teammates who welcomed her drive, energy, and kooky sense of fun. "It was honestly one of the best teams that I've ever been part of," she told a reporter years later.

Small and quick, with a mischievous playfulness, Carli earned a reputation as a lovable pain in the butt off the field. When she ran onto the field and took her position at center midfield, though, she was all seriousness.

Center midfielders are the link between the offensive forwards and the defenders. When a goalkeeper or defender clears the ball from their team's half of the field, the center middie helps move it toward the opponent's goal by dribbling or passing it up to the offense. She can attack the goal herself, too, if she gets the chance. When the ball heads toward her own goal, she switches to defense, plugging up holes, stealing the ball with careful tackles, and intercepting passes. It's a tough job that takes a lot of mental focus, heads-up play, and ball-handling skill.

Carli brought all that and something more to the field: a competitive drive that was off the charts! In 1996, when she was fourteen, her talent and desire to win earned her a spot in the Olympic Development Program, an organization that invites elite youth players to training camps, where their potential as future members of the US National Team is evaluated. She was excited by the idea that she might one day represent the United States on the international stage.

But when she got to the weeklong training camp at the University of Massachusetts Amherst, that excitement was replaced with other emotions. "I [was] a mess of nerves and anxiety the whole week," Carli confessed later.

As bad as her homesickness was, her crippling self-doubt was even worse. From almost the moment she arrived, she convinced herself that she didn't belong. That her skills were subpar compared to the other girls'. That *she* was subpar, and that there was no way she'd make the final roster of eighteen.

It's hard to perform your best when your mind is whispering that you don't stand a chance. When the roster came out, Carli's name wasn't on it.

For some players, two rejections in two years would be enough to crush their dreams for good. And Carli was crushed—no doubt about it. But she refused to let her dream die. Instead, she focused on the lesson she'd learned: training her feet and body weren't enough. To be the best player she could be, she had to work on her self-confidence, too.

She had a huge supporter in that area, a young teen named Brian Hollins, who years later would become her husband. The two started out as neighborhood friends, then began dating in high school. An athlete himself with a passion for golf—he joined the Philadelphia Professional Golfers' Association (PGA) after college—Brian understood Carli's drive to improve, to give soccer her all. He also knew she needed to learn to believe in herself. When those whispers of self-doubt crept into her mind, he stood ready to quiet them, something he still does for her today.

Fourteen-year-old Carli, now a freshman in high school, began to devote herself to soccer. Every fall for the next four years, she suited up for Delran High School as their center midfielder. Her impressive abilities and exciting style of play earned her statewide recognition. In 1999 and 2000, her junior and senior seasons, she was named High School Player of the Year by the *Philadelphia Inquirer* and to the *Parade* All-American Team. She was also the *Courier Post* Player of the Year and Burlington County Player of the Year, and in 2000, the choice of South Jersey Soccer Coaches Association for Midfielder of the Year. With Carli on the field, Delran High rocketed to an 18–3 record her senior year and a near-miss at winning the state tournament.

Those same four years, Carli continued playing for the Medford Strikers, helping lead the club to back-to-back state championships in 1997 and 1998. The club, and Carli in particular, received regular recognition in the sports section of local newspapers.

Word of the dynamic young midfielder began to reach the attention of college coaches. Soon, offers to come play for their schools poured in. Carli decided to play for the Scarlet Knights of Rutgers University because it was in her home state of New Jersey. Although she was a long way away from the homesick fourteen-year-old she used to be, going to school in a familiar area would no doubt make the transition from home to college easier.

It was a perfect fit right from the start. Carli made friends with the girls on the team and clicked with Coach Glenn Crooks. She not only rose to the new challenges of competing against top-notch teams around the mid-Atlantic region, she thrived on it. Crooks recognized her talent and gave her ample playing time her freshman year. She repaid his confidence by racking up an unbelievable season total of fifteen goals, assisting her teammates on seven others, and helping the Scarlet Knights to a stellar 14–8–1 record. She was named Rookie of the Year, an All-American athlete, and a First Team All-Big East selection.

Her impressive college career continued the following three years. As a sophomore, she drilled in twelve goals and seven assists for thirty-one points, earned her second All-American honor and First Team All-Big East selection, and was a semifinalist for the prestigious Hermann Trophy, given to the country's top college soccer player.

While earning these outstanding stats and nationwide recognition, Carli was simultaneously zeroing in on the next big step in her soccer career: the Under-21 Women's National Team. She made the squad in 2002 after her sophomore season. If she performed well, she had a shot at trying out for the full USWNT. That summer, she traveled with the U-21 team to Finland for the Nordic Cup, a small annual tournament for U-21 teams from Norway, Finland, Sweden, Germany, Denmark, Iceland, Canada, and the United States. She didn't end up playing many minutes, but the coach, Jerry Smith, liked her energy and her drive.

"Carli Lloyd isn't a finished product," he told others in the soccer community, "but she's got stuff you can't teach."

Carli returned to the weeklong U-21 training camp in January 2003. She'd just finished her junior season with Rutgers, another phenomenal effort that saw her chalking up twenty-eight points with thirteen goals and two assists and taking home her third All-American honor and First Team All-Big East selection. She arrived at camp feeling confident and ready.

Then she met the new head coach, Chris Petrucelli. Right from the start, she had trouble reading him. Did he like what he saw in her or not? Self-doubt set in and lingered through the later camps in March and April.

At the end of that third camp, she found out what Petrucelli thought of her. She was very talented, he said. But he questioned her fitness and her willingness to put in the extra work. Then he delivered the final blow: "I simply can't put you on the roster."

With that stinging assessment ringing in her ears, Carli returned to her room at the camp and broke down sobbing.

*I'm done*, she remembered thinking then. *I'm*

*completely* done. She called her parents back in Delran. Through her tears, she told them that she'd been cut from the team. Then she revealed she was contemplating giving up soccer for good.

Her parents were devastated. They'd been staunch supporters from the start, shelling out whatever money was needed to provide her with gear and team fees, traveling far and wide to tournaments, and bolstering her confidence when it dipped low. They knew it was her dream to play for Team USA. They believed it was a dream that could still come true. She just needed help getting there.

Her father believed he knew where to find that help: the Medford Strikers.

# CHAPTER 2
# 2003–2011

## SUCCESSES AND STRUGGLES

In 2003, Carli's younger brother, Stephen, was playing for the Medford Strikers, Carli's old club. Their father had been impressed by one of the team's trainers, a man named James Galanis. An Australian, Galanis had played soccer professionally in his home country before moving to southern New Jersey with his wife and opening the Universal Soccer Academy in 2000. One rain-soaked night not long after Carli's desperate phone call, her father approached James, who was stowing equipment in his car.

"My daughter needs your help," he said. He asked James to meet Carli and to train her if they hit it off.

James remembered Carli from her Medford days. He gave Stephen his card and told him to have Carli contact him.

Carli did—but not for months. During that time, she'd been invited to play on the U-21 team when a teammate was forced out with an injury. She accepted, hoping that she could change Coach Petrucelli's mind about her. But Petrucelli still wasn't a fan of her playing. So she went into her final season with Rutgers thinking she'd end her soccer career when the last game was over.

But something inside her wasn't quite ready to call it quits. So that December, after finishing as Rutgers number one all-time point earner (117) and goal scorer (50), Carli decided to contact James and set up a meeting for him to assess her skills.

It would turn out to be the best decision she'd ever made. Fifteen minutes into the evaluation, though, she regretted making it!

James put her through the most rigorous technical workout she'd ever experienced. Dribbling around poles, passing from foot to foot, shooting, anything and everything that demonstrated her footwork and control of the ball. "I almost had a heart attack!" Carli remembered.

The next day's assessment of her physical fitness was even more challenging. She ran. And sprinted. And ran some more. Over the grassy field, up hills, on the track, constant, continuous motion with no letting up. Only when she was done—heart pounding, gasping, sweaty even in the chill December air—did James explain his training philosophy, the Five Pillars: technical skill, tactical awareness, physical power, mental toughness, and character. He told Carli she excelled at the first two. But the other three? Those needed significant work if she ever wanted to achieve her dream of playing soccer on the world stage. He would train her, he said, but only if she committed herself 100 percent to the Five Pillars.

Carli thought it over for less than a second before giving him her answer: "I'm in."

They began almost immediately. The long, grueling workouts pushed Carli to her absolute max and left her exhausted physically, emotionally, and mentally. She loved it. Even when she was on the brink of collapse, James and his Five Pillars spoke to her as no other training regimen ever had. When the U-21 training camp rolled back around in January 2004, she was stronger, fitter, faster, and mentally tougher than she'd ever been in her life.

Coach Petrucelli noticed the changes she'd made. Noticed—and greatly approved. This time, when the roster came out, Carli's name was on it. In March 2004, she traveled with the team to China for her first match. When she scored a goal in that 4–0 victory, her confidence ticked up a notch. Finally, she dared to think, she was making an impact.

She was. Not long after the U-21 April training camp, she received a surprising and thrilling phone call. The voice on the other end belonged to April Heinrichs, coach of the USWNT. Heinrichs was calling to invite Carli to work out with the team.

Carli was beside herself with excitement. The players on the team—Mia Hamm, Kristine Lilly, Julie Foudy, Joy Fawcett, and Briana Scurry—were the rock stars of women's soccer, the winners of the 1999 Women's World Cup—the premier tournament of soccer, played every four years—and soon-to-be winners of the gold medal at the 2004 Summer Olympics in Athens. She knew she wasn't competing for a spot on the roster, but to share the field with players of that caliber was an honor all the same.

Soon after that camp, Carli graduated from Rutgers. She also accepted an offer to play for the New Jersey Wildcats, a professional team in the W-League, a women's soccer development organization. And she continued to train regularly with James Galanis, working on strengthening her skills as well as her body. The following January, Carli came to the US national team training camp ready to prove she belonged on the roster with those players. She'd been working with James for more than a year by then and had never felt stronger or more mentally prepared. The team's new coach, Greg Ryan, was impressed by her ball-handling skills, competitive attitude, and eagerness to give 110 percent. She made the team.

Carli could barely believe it. "It [was] almost as if a tidal wave of euphoria [was] going to sweep me away," she said of the moment she heard her name called.

On the team with her were Tiffeny Milbrett, Aly Wagner, Shannon Boxx, Abby Wambach, Shannon MacMillan, and Kristine Lilly, among others. Gone from the roster were stars Mia Hamm and Joy Fawcett, who had retired the previous year. Practices began soon after.

And so did Carli's struggles.

Coach Ryan had made it clear that he wanted to build the USWNT into a defensive powerhouse. As an attacking midfielder, Carli was much more comfortable and skilled at offense. She tried to do what Ryan asked of her—tightening up on opponents, closing open spaces, falling back instead of charging forward—but she started worrying that it wasn't enough. Even after she got her first cap—the soccer term referring to her first game with the national team—in a game versus Ukraine on July 10, 2005, she feared she'd spend more time on the bench than on the field.

She got a break from her concerns when she rejoined the U-21 team in late July for the Nordic Cup. (Per tournament rules, the team is allowed to take four players over the age of twenty-one.) The squad had a new coach named Jill Ellis, who had heard good things about Carli. "A one-man wrecking crew" was one college coach's assessment.

Carli helped the U-21 team to victories over Iceland, Denmark, and Germany before facing Norway in the final. There, she assisted on one goal in the second half and added one of her own to help Team USA beat Norway 4–1 and take their seventh consecutive Nordic Cup.

Despite her good showing in Iceland, Carli returned to the national team with a belly full of butterflies. Would she see any playing time? Or would Greg Ryan keep her on the bench in favor of a more defensive-minded player?

On the bench, it seemed, at least until the last game of 2005.

That October match was a friendly—the soccer term for a scrimmage, or a game played for fun to give the players experience—played in South Carolina against Mexico. In the second half and with a comfortable 3–0 lead, Carli subbed in for Wagner. She came close to assisting MacMillan on a goal, only to have the Mexican keeper rebuff MacMillan's shot. Carli got her own chance to score, but the keeper fended off that attempt, too.

Then, with just seconds left in the game, she got a second opportunity. She was far from the goal, but with the game basically won, she figured it was worth trying a shot. She drew her foot back, swung through, and *wham!* Her foot struck the ball but not in the way she'd intended. As the ball shot straight upward, she fell sideways. She'd put so much power into the kick that she lost her balance on the follow-through. Instinctively, she flung her arm out to break her fall. When she hit—*crack!* She knew even before getting the X-rays what had happened: She'd broken her wrist.

Fortunately, the break healed in time for the 2006 training camp in January. What hadn't healed was Carli's self-confidence. Her fear that she wasn't the kind of player Greg Ryan wanted continued to haunt her. His hot-and-cold attitude, praising her one second and harshly criticizing her the next, didn't help.

Nor did an explosive argument they had toward the end of the season. During a team meeting, Carli finally got the courage to speak her mind. She told Ryan she believed her defensive play had improved and that she thought she was doing well. In front of the other players, Ryan disagreed loudly, and with great anger. Later, he spoke to her alone, warning her that if she challenged him again when other players were present, she could pack her bags.

Carli saw little playing time in the 2006 season. She did her best to work through her disappointment and low self-esteem by redoubling her training efforts with James Galanis. More than anyone in her life, even more than her longtime boyfriend, Brian, James knew how to reach Carli when she needed a boost. Through texts and e-mails, phone calls and meetings, he reminded her that there was only one person she had total control over: herself.

"With a strong mind, you can become whatever you want to become," he once told her. Visualize your goals, he said, and you're on the way to making them happen.

Carli took that message to heart going into 2007, a year that saw the return of the Women's World Cup. Team USA had walked out with a third-place finish in the 2003 competition, a bitter disappointment to the players and fans after their triumph in 1999. This time, they hoped to return to the top.

First, though, came the Algarve Cup, an annual tournament held in mid-March in Portugal. The twelve participating teams were divided into three groups for the early group stage round. At the end of round-robin play—a format where each team in a group plays the other teams once—the US team was in first place in Group B, having defeated Finland, Sweden, and China. Per the rules of the tournament, that top rank automatically earned them a spot in the finals.

There, they faced off against the winner of Group A, Denmark. Carli went into the match feeling primed and ready. And with good reason: in each of the group stage games, she'd scored a goal—two of them game winners! Until this tournament, she had scored only one international goal in twenty-four appearances, so that was an impressive achievement. "I am going to continue to grow as a player and help this team as much as I can," she told reporters after the tournament.

And help she did! In the final, Team USA was up 1–0 thanks to a goal in the twelfth minute from Kristine Lilly. Six minutes into the second half, Carli collected the ball thirty yards out from Denmark's goal. She dribbled in a little closer, then *boom!* She walloped a powerful left-footed kick. The ball hit the crossbar, then ricocheted down behind the goal line with such force it rocketed back up and billowed the net!

The USWNT won the match 2–0, and the tournament. To no one's surprise, Carli was awarded Top Goal Scorer and MVP honors. When asked what spurred her breakout performance, Carli replied, "My confidence. . . . It's easier to get the job done."

Six months later, Carli and her teammates were looking to "get the job done" at the Women's World Cup in China. Held from September 10 to September 30, the tournament hosted sixteen teams divided into four groups for round-robin play. Carli hoped to duplicate her Algarve Cup performance and contribute more goals and scoring opportunities for her teammates. So she was excited to learn that she was in the starting lineup for the first game. She played well in the opener against Korea, though she was disappointed that the game ended in a 2–2 tie. She was more disappointed in the following match—not in the result, a 2–0 win over Sweden, but because Coach Ryan subbed her out midway through.

Team USA won their third game, too, 1–0, over Nigeria. But despite coming out on top in the group stage, Carli felt unsatisfied. The team wasn't jelling well, in her opinion, and she was frustrated by the number of missed opportunities, lackluster play, and poor focus.

She was even more frustrated with Coach Ryan. After the match, he showered her with praise, even called her the "future of the team"—and then told her she'd be sitting out the start of the game against England. When the United States won that match, he told her she'd sit out the start of the next, against Brazil. And then, when the team failed to survive the semifinals, falling to Brazil 4–0, she sat out the entire third-place match against Norway.

The season ended shortly afterward. Carli realized she had a choice to make: accept her role as a substitute or dig deeper, train harder, and work her way back into the starting lineup. She chose to work, and as always, James Galanis was right there with her. She spent hours every day strengthening her body, increasing her flexibility and speed, and focusing on her mental toughness. When the 2008 season began, she was ready for a fresh start.

That start was a little easier to make because Team USA had a new coach. After the loss to Brazil, Greg Ryan was replaced with Pia Sundhage. Carli was excited by Sundhage's ideas for turning the team into an attacking offensive. Sundhage believed that the midfield, and Carli in particular, would play a crucial role in that new approach.

Helping her bring this vision to life was her assistant coach, and Carli's former U-21 coach, Jill Ellis. With Sundhage and Ellis at the helm, playing soccer was fun again.

And so was preparing for the 2008 Summer Olympics in China.

Team USA had won the gold four years earlier and wanted nothing more than to defend their title. They looked in good position to do that, especially after winning their eighth consecutive Algarve Cup, where Carli chalked up another goal early in the tournament and assisted on the game winner in the final match.

Fast-forward four months to the Beijing Olympics, though, and it was a very different story for the defending gold-medal champions. The United States took the field without their number one scoring threat, Abby Wambach, who had suffered a horrifying leg injury in a match three weeks earlier. And when the game started, Norway came out hard and fast. Two minutes in—*bam!* Leni Larsen Kaurin headed the ball past Hope Solo. Two minutes after that—*boot!* Melissa Wiik followed up with a quick-touch goal off a bobbled back pass. Two goals in four minutes—it was the fastest any team had ever scored in the Olympics. Stunned, Team USA couldn't answer. Final score: Norway 2, USA 0.

The team was devastated and embarrassed by the loss, their first ever in group play. But while they were down, they weren't out. And Carli was the reason why. In the twenty-seventh minute of their next game, versus Japan, she collected the ball on a cross from teammate Stephanie Cox and drilled it into the net. No one else scored. Final result: USA 1, Japan 0.

The last match of group play was a 4–0 victory over New Zealand. Next up: the quarterfinals versus Canada. The USWNT got on the board first.

Then a violent thunder and lightning storm interrupted the game for a full ninety minutes. When play finally resumed, Team USA took the win to reach the semifinals.

There, they faced off against Japan. The Japanese surprised them by scoring in the sixteenth minute. They held the 1–0 lead until the final minutes of the first half. Then—*boom! Pow!* The US team scored back-to-back goals! They added a third and fourth in the second half, and while Japan did their best to overcome the deficit, they could only put one more past Solo. Final score: USA 4, Japan 2. Team USA was in the finals!

But so was Brazil. It was the second consecutive Olympic gold-medal matchup between the two powerhouses. In 2004, the two had battled to a 1–1 tie that sent the game into extra minutes. When Abby Wambach of Team USA had scored, Brazil went home in defeat. They did not want the same result in 2008.

To get her head in the right space, Carli thought about something James Galanis had written in a recent email: *Work the hardest, concentrate the most, and be ready for anything.*

From the get-go, Brazil came out strong, with

their star scorers, Marta and Cristiane, attacking the goal again and again. But Hope Solo was on fire, delivering amazing saves, including a one-armed diving block that deflected Marta's kick from point-blank range.

The game stayed scoreless throughout the first half. And the second. And the first six minutes of overtime.

That's when Team USA worked the ball down into Brazil's territory. Carli collected a short pass from Lauren Cheney. Under pressure, she back-heeled the ball to Amy Rodriguez. Rodriguez sent it back almost immediately. Carli took a single touch to put the ball in open space. Followed it. Then—

"I just thought, *Go*," she remembered. With a pinpoint-accurate left-footed blast, she drilled the ball past Brazil's keeper and into the back right corner!

"When I saw the ball hit the net, I was sort of in shock," she said.

She nearly added a second goal toward the end of overtime, but that kick clanged off the post. But it didn't matter. Her single score was enough. When time ran out, Team USA was the gold medalist!

Carli was beyond thrilled by the win and to be

named the US Soccer Female Player of the Year by the US Soccer Federation. But she wasn't about to sit back and relax. That just wasn't her style. Besides, as James reminded her with a statement written large on a blackboard at his training facility: THE OLYMPICS ARE FORGOTTEN. Meaning, you've accomplished something amazing, but it's what you do next that matters.

For Carli, what came next was exploring a career with the new Women's Professional Soccer (WPS) league. The league wanted star players to help bolster attendance, and after her performance in the Olympics, Carli was definitely that!

She started her WPS career with the Chicago Red Stars in 2009, then moved back home to play for Sky Blue FC in New Jersey in 2010. Unfortunately, she suffered a major setback early in the 2010 season. During a match against the Red Stars, she slipped and landed awkwardly on her left ankle, breaking it.

Recovering from the injury tested her patience. "It wasn't easy," Carli admitted. "I had to take baby steps."

Carli pushed through her rehabilitation and, by the end of July, was back on the field, this time with the USWNT. Team USA was preparing for the Confederation of North, Central American, and Caribbean Association Football (CONCACAF) qualifiers, the tournament that determined which teams from that region would advance to the 2011 Women's World Cup.

"Everybody figured we'd waltz through qualifying," Carli said. And they did in the group stage, beating Haiti 5–0, Guatemala 9–0, and Costa Rica 4–0. But in the semifinals, Mexico stunned them by pulling off a 2–1 win. Carli made the lone goal that match, but the loss forced the team into a two-game playoff with Italy. Whichever team came out with the most goals after those two games would have a berth in the 2011 World Cup. The other team would go home.

Luckily, Team USA pulled out a 1–0 win in Padua, Italy, and another 1–0 victory in Illinois. Now it was time to set their sights on the big prize: the World Cup.

That prize came close to slipping through Team USA's fingers when they dropped a game to Sweden in the group stage and nearly lost to Brazil in the quarterfinals of the knockout round. A truly epic, game-winning header by Abby Wambach saved them that day. With a decisive 3–1 win over France in the semifinals, they advanced to the finals.

There, they faced Japan, a team they had beaten nearly every time they'd met in the last two decades. But this year's Japanese team was tougher, faster, and stronger than those of the past. After a scoreless first half, the United States got on the board with a goal from newcomer Alex Morgan. Japan answered with one of their own minutes before the end of regulation time, knotting it up at 1–1 and sending the game into its first overtime.

Both teams scored a single goal. The 2011 Women's World Cup would be decided by a penalty kick shoot-out.

Penalty kick shoot-outs are one of the most exciting, stressful experiences in sports, both for the players and the fans. Five players from each team are selected to take shots against the goalkeeper—no defenders, no help from teammates, just one on one, kicker versus keeper. The teams alternate kickers, and whichever team scores the most penalty kicks wins.

"You're wondering, does the goalkeeper know where you're going? Do you hit it harder or softer?"

Carli said. "All these mixed emotions going through your head."

Japan's keeper, Ayumi Kaihori, made three saves out of the five US kicks and allowed just one ball into the net. There was one kick that Kaihori didn't have to save, though, because the ball rocketed high over the crossbar. The person who kicked that ball?

Carli Lloyd.

"I overhit it," she remembered.

The Japanese drilled their last two penalty kicks past Hope Solo. They won the game—and became the new World Cup champions.

Carli was absolutely devastated by the loss, especially the part she played in the missed penalty kick.

It was a feeling she never wanted to have again. So, she did what she always did.

She got to work.

# CHAPTER 3
# 2012–2019

## GOLDEN GLORY

After their World Cup loss, Carli and Team USA returned home to an unexpected reception. Even though they'd come in second, "We were being cheered," Carli remembered. "Everyone was cheering for us."

Buoyed by the outpouring of support, Carli pushed herself even harder in training, in practices, and during friendlies, digging deeper to give just a little bit more. Her teammates worked with equal determination because in less than a year, they'd be taking the field looking to defend their 2008 Olympic title.

No one wanted to come home with a second gold medal more than Carli Lloyd. So when Coach Sundhage started Shannon Boxx in the first match instead of her—Boxx and teammate Lauren Cheney (later Holiday, after her marriage) had been working well together—Carli wasn't happy. But in the seventeenth minute, Boxx pulled a hamstring. Carli subbed in for her.

Team USA was down 0–2 then. A header by Abby Wambach in the eighteenth minute made it 1–2. Alex Morgan tied it up shortly after that. That's where the score stayed until nine minutes into the second half. Then Megan Rapinoe captured the ball near the right sideline and raced with it toward France's goal. Carli followed, ready for a pass. It came. She dribbled forward. Around a defender. And then *boom!* She blasted a kick that sent the ball sailing into the net. Team USA had their first lead of the game. They sweetened it with one more goal. Final score: USA 4, France 2.

Carli posted another goal in the 3–0 win over Colombia. She didn't score in the next three games, but her teammates did—enough to send them to the finals.

Their opponents in that match? The team that beat them in the 2011 World Cup: Japan.

Carli couldn't wait for the rematch. When she jogged onto the field for the gold-medal game, she felt prepared, energized, and confident.

And a confident Carli Lloyd was always a danger to opponents.

Almost from the opening whistle, Carli was on the attack. In the eighth minute, Alex Morgan nabbed the ball just before it bounced over Japan's goal line. With a full-body twist, she threaded a high pass from the left of Japan's goal over to the right. Carli and Abby Wambach were both near the right of the box. They were hungry to score. Abby flashed out a leg, reaching for the ball. Carli charged forward at the same time, head down. A split second later—*swish!* The ball landed in the net! At first, it looked as though Wambach had scored. But on closer inspection, it was clear Carli's head had driven the ball past the Japanese keeper.

"Abby and I actually joked that I stole her goal," Carli said.

USA 1, Japan 0.

That's where the score stayed until seven minutes into the second half. Then Megan Rapinoe collected the ball just over the midfield line. She saw Carli racing down the center of the field and booted her a pass. Carli dribbled forward—and kept going, veering right until she was just within firing range. Without breaking stride, she drilled the ball over three defenders, past the keeper, and into the net!

"What a goal by Carli Lloyd!" cried the announcer. "Virtuoso stuff!"

But the game wasn't over yet, as Japan proved when they hit the strings behind Hope Solo to make it 2–1. Carli nearly scored again, only to watch the ball fly over the crossbar. Then Solo prevented a tie with a diving save.

With the final minutes ticking away, the Japanese made their most aggressive attack yet. Too aggressive—an overzealous player tripped Carli inside USA's box. The ref called a foul and awarded Solo a free kick.

Solo sent that ball on a journey far downfield. And that's where it stayed until the final whistle blasts. Team USA once again won Olympic gold!

Carli Lloyd was now thirty years old. She'd been playing soccer for twenty-five years, had two Olympic gold medals, and had played in more than one hundred international matches, including two World Cups. Some players might look on that lofty career and decide it was time to retire.

Carli did the opposite. With James Galanis and his Five Pillars guiding her, she trained harder than ever to stay in peak physical condition. And she played for her new WPS team—the same squad

James was now coaching, the Atlanta Beat. Her time there was short, however, for the WPS folded at the end of 2012. A year later, she found a spot closer to home on the Western New York Flash of the newly created National Women's Soccer League.

And of course, she trained with Team USA throughout those years, focusing on their next goal: capturing the World Cup in 2015.

There were some bumps along the way to that goal, though. Pia Sundhage left at the end of 2012 to coach for Sweden, her native country. Not long after, Carli learned that Joe Dadura, her old Medford Strikers coach, had passed away. That mental blow was followed by a physical one, a shoulder injury sustained during the 2013 Algarve Cup. She was forced to sit out for more than two months while it healed. Then a year later, Tom Sermanni, the USWNT coach who had replaced Sundhage, was fired after a disastrous 2014 Algarve Cup.

There were two very bright moments for Carli in those same years, however. One was in January 2013, when her longtime boyfriend, Brian Hollins, asked her to marry him. (She said yes!) The other was in 2014, when she learned that the new coach for Team USA was Jill Ellis. "Jill is the perfect fit for us. She's smart, knowledgeable, and experienced," Carli said, "and though she is friendly and approachable, she is nobody's pushover."

The team was no pushover, either. Team USA hosted the CONCACAF qualifiers in mid-October 2014. After a wobbly 1–0 start against Trinidad and Tobago in the group stage, Team USA romped over Guatemala 5–0 and Haiti 6–0. Carli contributed goals in those two games—and two more in the semifinal victory over Mexico. Abby Wambach tore the field up in the 6–0 finals against Costa Rica with four goals, and Carli added one as well.

More important, though, Carli played outstanding ball throughout the tournament. In recognition of her contributions, she was awarded the Golden Ball, which is given to the best player throughout the tournament.

More training, practicing, and friendlies filled the months after the qualifiers. Then suddenly, the 2015 World Cup was upon them. Twenty-four teams, up from the previous sixteen, traveled to Canada for the monthlong summer tournament. After the group stage, knockout round, and quarterfinals, only four teams remained: Germany, England, Japan, and the United States. The United States beat Germany 2–0, with Carli contributing one of those goals on a penalty kick. And when Japan beat England 2–1, fans around the world prepared for a thrilling rematch between the rival powerhouses.

They got more than they bargained for, all thanks to Carli Lloyd.

In the third minute, Carli deflected a perfectly placed corner kick from Megan Rapinoe into the net. USA 1, Japan 0.

In the fifth minute, Carli sprinted past two Japanese defenders and side-kicked the ball into the net. USA 2, Japan 0.

And then came the kick seen round the world. The kick that vaulted Carli Lloyd into soccer history. In the sixteenth minute, just two minutes after teammate Lauren Holiday scored, Carli collected the ball at midfield. She dribbled forward. She looked up and saw keeper Ayumi Kaihori out of the goal. She drew back her foot and—*BOOM!*— hammered the ball, sending it on a soaring journey half the length of the field...and into the net! It was hands down the most audacious and unbelievable goal ever seen in a World Cup final. USA 4, Japan 0.

"Are you even human?" was all Hope Solo could say as she gave Carli a fierce hug after that goal.

Seventy-four minutes of play later, the United

States won their first World Cup since 1999. Carli was named Player of the Match. She also received the Golden Ball and the Silver Boot for having scored six goals and assisted on one other.

That night, after a joyful on-field celebration, the team received a phone call from the president of the United States, Barack Obama. After congratulating the players as a whole, he singled out the tournament's star. "And Carli? What have you been eating?" he joked. "I wanna do what you're doing!"

What Carli had been doing, what she'd been doing for years, was working hard to be the best. And just because she'd earned that title in the World Cup, she wasn't about to take a step back. The 2016 Olympics were less than a year away, after all, and Team USA had a title to defend.

But sadly, Carli, now a team captain, and her teammates lost their chance to repeat as gold medalists when their quarterfinal game against Sweden came down to a penalty kick shoot-out. Three of their five shots, including one from Carli, found the back of the net. But four of Sweden's got past Hope Solo. For the first time ever, the United States would not advance to the semifinals.

"It's always hard to swallow losing in [penalty kicks]," Carli said after the loss. "[But] this team is not going to crumble."

It didn't. But the team did change over the next few years. The coaches tweaked the lineup, adding new, younger players to the roster and testing current players in different positions.

As a veteran player with more than a decade of experience, Carli had been through such changes before. She understood that for the team to be successful, the coaches needed to bring in fresh talent and try new lineups. As a team captain, she encouraged the newcomers to give their all every time they stepped onto the field. She led by example, pushing herself to run faster, pass smarter, and kick harder. She reminded them and everyone on the team that the 2019 Women's World Cup was approaching; if they wanted to repeat as champions, they needed to be at their peak level of performance.

In short, Carli gave Team USA her all in the months leading up to the World Cup. Which is why it came as a blow when she learned she wouldn't be a starter in the first match of the tournament. When reporters asked Coach Ellis why, she explained that right now, Carli was more valuable as a strong backup than as a starter.

Carli wasn't ready to be benched. Not by a long shot.

"At the end of the day," she told a reporter before the World Cup, "I can help this team lift that trophy in France."

Now playing backup forward, a wholly offensive position, rather than midfielder, Carli came off the bench in the first game of group play, against Thailand, and scored a goal in overtime. She started in the next match versus Chile—and booted in not one but two goals. Those goals made her the only player to score in six consecutive World Cup games.

While Carli didn't score again, she was instrumental to the team whenever she was on the field. And when she wasn't, she was fully focused on the action and supported her teammates.

That was particularly true in the finals, where Team USA faced the Netherlands. Carli prowled the sidelines, watching as her teammates battled the Dutch through the first minutes of play, hoping Team USA would continue its five-game streak of scoring a goal within the first twelve minutes.

It didn't, but they came close to getting on the

board when Alex Morgan deflected a cross from Megan Rapinoe toward the goal. But the Dutch keeper made the save. Two minutes later, she stopped another shot by Morgan. The Dutch couldn't put one past Team USA's Alyssa Naeher, either. Going into the break, both teams were scoreless.

That changed after sixty minutes, when Morgan took a high kick to the shoulder from a Dutch player inside the Netherlands' penalty box. The kick was ruled a foul. The United States was awarded a penalty kick. When Rapinoe buried the ball in the net to give Team USA its first goal, Carli was as excited as anyone else.

More minutes ticked by with neither team adding points to their side of the board. Then, in the sixty-ninth minute, Rose Lavelle, one of the younger players on Team USA, got possession of the ball at half field. Before her was open space. She took off, dribbling straight for the goal. Two Dutch defenders charged toward her. She sidestepped one, then blasted a kick from the top of the box. The Dutch keeper dove to make the save—but missed!

The United States was still up 2–0 when Carli came in at the eighty-seven-minute mark. The game was all but over by then, but she played the way she always played: as hard as she could and with complete focus. And when the final whistle sounded, she was right in the thick of the team's victory hug.

Three years earlier, Team USA had returned home with their heads hung low. This time, they carried them—and the World Cup trophy—high amid the cheers and applause of their fans.

For Carli, the victory was a tremendous highlight in a long and storied career. "I feel like the old granny a little bit," she joked during a speech in New York City after a celebratory ticker-tape parade. After thanking everyone who had supported them through the months, she smiled her 100-watt smile. "Here's to the next chapter. Maybe we'll see you in another four years."

If the team is lucky enough to fill their roster with hardworking, dedicated players like Carli Lloyd, chances are good they will be back.

As for Carli's own future, it's not clear yet exactly what it will hold. She is active in both the Medford Strikers club and James Galanis's Universal Soccer Academy, giving talks to young players about mental toughness and holding training clinics. She garnered a lot of press in the fall of 2019 when she nailed a fifty-five-yard field goal during a practice session with the Philadelphia Eagles of the National Football League, and she's finding time to play golf with her husband, Brian.

And there is soccer. At thirty-seven years old, she knows the younger members of the USWNT and her NWSL team—a hometown New Jersey girl, she's now back with Sky Blue—will continue to claim more playing time. But she's as fit and determined as ever to keep a foot in the game she loves.

"I want to enjoy it," she recently said of the time she has left playing. Then she added with a smile, "But there isn't a day where I'm going to stop fighting."

# CARLI LLOYD'S CAREER HIGHLIGHTS

**2005**

First US Women's National Team appearance, July 10

**2006**

First US Women's National Team goal, October 1

**2007**

FIFA Women's World Cup: Bronze Medal

**2008**

Beijing Olympics: Gold Medal
US Soccer Female Player of the Year

**2010**

Played 100th cap, November 27

**2011**

FIFA Women's World Cup: Silver Medal

**2012**

London Olympics: Gold Medal

## 2015

Played 200th cap, June 26

FIFA Women's World Cup: Gold Medal

First player in history to score a hat trick in
    under sixteen minutes in a final

FIFA Women's World Cup Golden Ball

FIFA Women's World Cup Silver Boot

FIFA Women's World Cup Goal of the
    Tournament

FIFA World Player of the Year

## 2016

Rio Olympics: Fifth Place

FIFA World Player of the Year

## 2018

Scored 100th goal, April 8

## 2019

First player in history to score in six consecutive
    Women's World Cup games

FIFA Women's World Cup: Gold Medal

ESPY Award: Best Team

# ALEX MORGAN

Alex Morgan fights for the ball during the 2019 Women's World Cup final against the Netherlands.

Romain Biard/Shutterstock.com

Alex Morgan controls the ball during a Tournament of Nations game against Australia on July 29, 2018.

Lev Radin/Shutterstock.com

Romain Biard/Shutterstock.com

# CHAPTER 1
# 1989–2008

## FROM ALI CAT TO BABY HORSE

When Alex Morgan was eight years old, she left her mother a Post-it Note. "Hi Mommy! My name is Alex and I am going to be a professional athlete for soccer. I love you!" She signed it with her nickname, Ali Cat.

Twelve years later, Alex Morgan had a new nickname: Baby Horse. Her teammates had given it to her. Horse, because of how she looked when she ran, all long legs and longer strides. And Baby because at just twenty years old, she was the youngest member of the United States Women's National Team (USWNT).

Alex had been captivated by the team in 1999 when they won the World Cup. Then she watched them win back-to-back gold medals at the 2004 and 2008 Olympics. And now, unbelievably, she was playing with Kristine Lilly, Christie Rampone,

Abby Wambach, Carli Lloyd, and other soccer greats as equals.

It was everything she'd ever dreamed of, but it was just the beginning.

Alexandra Morgan was supposed to be Alexan*der* Morgan. Her parents, Michael and Pam, already had two daughters, Jeni and Jeri, and just assumed their third child would be a boy. So when Alex was born on July 2, 1989, her father decided she'd have to be the son he never had. He was joking, of course, but when Alex showed an early interest in sports, he couldn't have been happier. And when she announced she liked soccer, he helped her practice in the backyard and even coached her first teams.

Unlike many soccer greats who start training as young as age five, Alex didn't start playing serious ball until she was a young teenager. Instead, she played every sport available in her hometown of Diamond Bar, California.

"Basketball, tetherball, kickball, anything. I loved tetherball," she said with a laugh. "I was tetherball queen."

Soccer was a big part of her sports world, too. She played on American Youth Soccer Organization

(AYSO) teams throughout elementary and middle school. "I was one of those kids who wanted the soccer ball at all times and was going to push some people to get that ball," she remembered.

She loved being part of the AYSO teams. But as soccer became more and more important to her, Alex realized she needed to move to a more challenging league if she wanted to improve. So when she turned thirteen, she tried out for her first club soccer team. She knew it would be tough going up against girls who had been in the club circuit for years.

And it was. She didn't make the cut.

"For me to not even make the team, I was like...wow," she said.

Alex didn't let that setback keep her down. She tried out for another club, the Cypress Elite, the following year—and made it. Her coach, Dave Sabet, saw something special in her right from the start. "She had the makings of a great player," he remembered. But she wasn't quite there yet.

Sabet helped Alex hone her abilities. They worked on dribbling, ball control, shooting, passing, and more. She thrived under his tutelage, and soon her newfound soccer skills combined with her own natural abilities made her a force to be reckoned with on the field. "The girls weren't physically fast enough to keep up with Alex," Sabet once said. And she still had a hunger for the ball. Given the chance, she would collect a pass, attack the goal, and turn scoring opportunities into points for her team.

Her speed, scoring accuracy, and heads-up play did not go unnoticed. Just six months after joining the Cypress Elite, she was invited to the Cal South Olympic Development Program (ODP) camp. The purpose of the ODP is "to identify players of the highest caliber" and train them with the hopes that someday they'll make up the most competitive national team possible. To be chosen for the ODP was a huge step forward in Alex's soccer journey. "It made me realize I was a serious competitor," she remembered.

But as honored as Alex was to be part of the ODP, and as much as she loved being on the Cypress Elite as well as the Diamond Bar High School varsity team, she wasn't quite ready to give up other sports. Her freshman and sophomore year in high school, she played volleyball and ran track.

Looking back, Alex believes playing other sports helped her retain her passion for soccer instead of burning out. Unfortunately, volleyball and club soccer seasons overlapped. When she started missing practices for one or the other, Alex had to make a choice. She chose soccer.

With every passing year, Alex grew as a player. Good coaches and supportive parents were a big reason why. But it was Alex's hard work, dedication, and drive that really made the difference.

In 2007, at the age of seventeen, her push to improve and be the best she could be paid off. She made the US Under-20 Women's National Team. By that time, she'd helped the Cypress Elite win the Cal South Cup; was on her way to earning top high school athletic honors, including All-American; and had been accepted to the University of California, Berkeley, where she'd earned a spot in the Golden Bears lineup. She was excited to get to know her new teammates at Cal and on the U-20 team and play with other highly skilled players.

Unfortunately, she was sidelined early on from both teams. Not because she wasn't performing well. But because she was on crutches.

In the winter of her senior year, Alex and her U-20 teammates were scrimmaging their counterparts on the U-20 men's team when she fell. "I felt a sharp pain tear through my right knee," she recalled.

Diagnosis: a torn ACL, one of the major ligaments of the knee. Surgery repaired the damage, but if Alex was to return to the field, she'd have to endure long weeks of painful rehabilitation.

She readily rose to the challenge. Playing soccer in college and beyond had become a dream of hers. So she went to rehab sessions every week and attended high school and club practices even though she couldn't play.

"It was probably the best thing that happened for me, mentally," she said once. "It made me think a lot more about how much I loved the game."

Five months later, Alex was back on the field, wearing a Golden Bears uniform along with a protective knee brace. Some players might have eased their way back into the game after such an injury. Not Alex. She came out fighting. "She wasn't shy going into tackles," said her college coach, Neil McGuire. "Very committed and very aggressive." Photos showing Alex laid out, her right knee bent back as she slides in for a tackle with her left, are proof of her coach's statement.

A sprained ankle early in the season kept her on the Golden Bears bench for a few weeks. But her first game back, she scored a goal. The moment the ball hit the back of the net, it was as if her injuries had never happened. She jumped sky-high over and over, screaming with joy.

That first goal was followed by forty-four more in the four years she played for the Golden Bears. She finished her senior season as the third-highest point earner and goal scorer in the university's history. With Alex on the roster, UC Berkeley reached the National Collegiate Athletic Association (NCAA) tournament four years in a row. In recognition for her outstanding play, she was named to the All-Pac-10— given to top athletes from NCAA colleges in the Pacific region—four times and received Pac-10 All-Academic honorable mentions three times. She was nominated for the Hermann Trophy twice and once for the Honda Sports Award, given to the top women college athletes based on votes from coaches.

When not playing for the Golden Bears, Alex was wearing number 13, the number Kristine Lilly (her favorite player) wore, for the U-20 WNT. No player's spot is assured on any WNT from year to year, but Alex had been invited to the training camp again at the end of 2007. Though she hadn't performed well then, she made the 2008 squad when another player dropped out.

In late 2008, she and her teammates traveled to Chile to take part in the FIFA U-20 Women's World Cup, a tournament many soccer followers see as the best first look at the sport's future players. What they saw when Alex Morgan hit the field made them sit up and take notice.

Team USA's first game was on November 19 against France. In the front line with Alex was her teammate and friend, Sydney Leroux. Together, they packed a one-two offensive punch, with Alex delivering the first blow in the fifty-third minute. Leroux added two more goals in the 3–0 victory. That was the score when the United States beat Argentina, too, only this time, it was Alex who scored twice after teammate Becky Edwards put one in the net.

Three goals in two games? That was an impressive World Cup debut for the nineteen-year-old!

And she wasn't done yet. Although the United States lost to China in the group stage, they reached the finals after defeating England 3–0 in the quarter-finals and squeaking out a 1–0 win over Germany in the semifinals. Their opponent in the championship was North Korea. Nerves played a part in the early minutes of the match, with missed passes and botched opportunities on both sides.

Team USA got on the board first with another goal by Leroux. A second goal followed. The player who scored it? Alex Morgan.

In the forty-second minute, she beat out a defender for the ball in North Korea's territory. She used a combination of superior speed and precision dribbling to edge closer to the goal. Another defender swept in and interrupted the play with a sliding tackle. The ball took an awkward bounce, but Alex didn't falter. She recovered, dribbled to the top of the circle, and launched a left-footed blast so powerful it threw her off-balance. But even before she hit the ground, the ball flew into the back of the net!

Alex popped back to her feet, an incredulous but overjoyed grin lighting up her face, as her teammates swarmed her.

"A brilliant goal, worthy of a final" was how FIFA described the shot they later awarded Goal of the Tournament and second-best Goal of the Year. North Korea put one past Team USA's keeper in injury time, but it was too little too late. Thanks to Alex Morgan's incredible athleticism and scoring prowess, the U-20 team was the World Cup champ! Leroux was awarded the Golden Ball as the tournament's top player as well as the Golden Shoe for the most goals scored. Alex came home with the Silver Ball and the Bronze Shoe.

"I could hardly believe it," Alex remembered about that U-20 World Cup win in her autobiography, *Breakaway: Beyond the Goal*. But her dreams didn't stop there. "I wanted to join the US Women's National Team, and I wanted us to win a World Cup, too."

# CHAPTER 2
# 2009–2011

## CHAMPION ON THE RISE

Almost one year after her trailblazing performance in Chile, the first part of that dream came true. Thanksgiving morning, Alex was with her family in Diamond Bar when her phone rang. The general manager of the senior national team was on the other end—and inviting Alex to come train with the team after the holiday! Alex immediately accepted.

Unfortunately, that December camp didn't go as she hoped. A hamstring injury sidelined her on the third day; by the fourth, she was done with training for the next few weeks. After plenty of rest and some rehab, she worked her way back into peak form and returned to the team.

Alex played her first game as a member of the USWNT on March 31, 2010. The team was playing a friendly against Mexico in Sandy, Utah. But the stadium was anything but sandy—it was covered in ankle-deep snow, and more snow was coming down!

Prior to the match, Abby Wambach joked that if they scored, they would all make snow angels.

Alex had no clue if Wambach was serious—until Abby scored and immediately hurried to a spot near the corner of the field, lay down, and began flailing her arms and legs in the snow. Laughing, Alex and her teammates did the same. "There I was near Abby, freezing to death in three inches of powder," Alex remembered. "I thought I'd died and gone to heaven."

She was even happier seven months later. The team was playing a friendly against China in Pennsylvania on October 6. Team USA was down 0–1 in the eighty-second minute. They got possession and went on the attack. Abby and Alex charged downfield, both marked by defenders and both looking for a pass. A high-flying ball soared toward Abby. She controlled it, dropped it to the ground, and booted it into open space in front of Alex. Alex took two steps and—*blam!*—blasted it into the net!

"Alex Morgan!" the announcer cried. "Her first international goal is a beauty!"

It was a tie game, and when neither team scored

in the remaining time, the match ended in a draw. If not for Alex's goal, Team USA would have lost—the first defeat they would have had on their own soil in six years. What did Alex remember of that moment? "I was the happiest I've been in my life."

And she was happier still when she got to make a special phone call to her parents a short while later. She had just attended a team meeting where Coach Pia Sundhage announced the roster for the upcoming Confederation of North, Central American, and Caribbean Association Football (CONCACAF) qualifiers. Her name was on the list! "I am so proud of you," her mother said when Alex gave them the news. "You did it!"

Alex added her second and third goals at the CONCACAF qualifiers. But her most significant goal came on November 20, 2010.

Team USA had been forced to play two additional games, both against Italy, after failing to place first or second at the qualifiers. Whichever team came out on top in the playoff would advance to the World Cup. The loser would go home without a berth.

For Alex and her teammates, elimination from the World Cup was unthinkable. But the Italians were just as hungry for a slot. The teams battled for forty-five scoreless minutes on the field in Padua, Italy. Then forty more without either putting the ball in the net. Deciding that fresh legs might give Team USA an advantage, Coach Sundhage signaled for Alex to go in for Amy Rodriguez in the eighty-sixth minute.

"Just go to [the] goal," Sundhage told her. "You don't have to be tricky, you don't have to be smart, just go to [the] goal, because you're faster than everybody else."

The final four minutes of regulation time passed with no goals scored. Then three more minutes had been added on for injury time. Near the ninety-three-minute mark, the United States took a throw-in.

And Alex did what Sundhage had told her to do: She went to the goal. Carli Lloyd booted a high-flying ball deep into Italy's territory. Abby Wambach batted it down with a crisp header. The ball bounced toward the goal. Alex charged forward and—*pow!*—slammed a line drive right-footer past the keeper!

Final score: USA 1, Italy 0. That was the score at the end of the next game, too. By the skin of their teeth, Team USA had made it into the 2011 Women's World Cup.

Alex returned to California to celebrate the holidays—and her outstanding performance with Team USA—with her friends and family. In mid-January 2011, they all had something else to celebrate: Alex had been chosen by the Western New York Flash as the number one draft pick in the Women's Professional Soccer (WPS) league. While her time with the Flash was short-lived—the WPS folded the next year—being the first-round pick was a sign that her soccer stardom was rising.

Her performance during the 2011 Algarve Cup sent it even higher. She scored two goals in the third match of the annual March tournament in Team USA's 4–0 win over Finland and added another goal in the final. Those three tied her with teammate Carli Lloyd and Welsh player Jessica Fishlock for most goals, earning her a Silver Boot. More important, her continued contributions to the team's victories instilled her with self-confidence and filled her teammates with trust in her abilities, especially in the clutch.

And Alex's clutch plays were definitely needed in

the 2011 Women's World Cup. Germany hosted the sixteen-team tournament, played from June 26 to July 17. In past Cups, the United States had come out on top of their group during the first rounds. This year, they finished second behind Sweden, who beat them in the third group match. They survived the nail-biter quarterfinal round against Brazil, thanks to an amazing, game-tying header by Abby Wambach followed by a penalty shoot-out that saw Team USA score on all five attempts for the win.

Then came the semifinals against France. Team USA got on the board first with a quick goal from Lauren Cheney. But France evened it up ten minutes into the second half. That's when Coach Sundhage decided it was time for some changes. Out came Amy Rodriguez. In went Alex Morgan.

On the field, Alex kept her eyes open and her legs moving, looking for an opportunity to make an impact. Another crucial header from Wambach off a perfect corner kick from Cheney put Team USA up by one and energized the players. If they could just get one more, they'd feel even better.

As the ball was booted from one half of the field to the other, Alex danced past the midfield line in France's territory, watching and waiting. Then a long ball reached Wambach. She headed it on the ground to Megan Rapinoe. Rapinoe quickly kicked it to an open teammate—Alex Morgan.

Alex exploded into action. She raced to France's goal, dribbling past defenders. France's keeper came out to challenge. Alex didn't break stride. *Pow!* From the left corner of the box, she drilled the ball and—

"Oh! It's a splendid goal!" the announcer bellowed.

Final score: USA 3, France 1.

With a chance to help Team USA reclaim the title they'd last held in 1999, Alex couldn't wait to get on the field for the match against Japan. But she had to wait—as usual, she was being reserved for the second half of the game. When she did step onto the field after the break, she felt fresh, energized, and raring to do whatever it took to break the 0–0 tie. She nearly did just that in the forty-ninth minute with a quick shot off a cross from Heather O'Reilly. Disappointingly, the ball clanged off the post instead of into the net.

Twenty minutes later, though—*boom!* Rapinoe belted a long ball from the Team USA's half down to Japan's. The only US player anywhere near it was Alex. She beat out a defender for the ball and dribbled to the top of the penalty box. The defender matched her step for step.

Almost.

Seconds before the defender slid into a tackle, Alex kicked a left-footer. The ball flew on a line—and into the goal!

"Is this a dream?" Alex remembered thinking. "When I heard the crowd explode, I knew it was real."

Alex's goal helped boost the team to new levels of play. But at the end, the day—and the World Cup trophy—went to Japan. The overtime match ended in a tie, forcing a penalty kick shoot-out. Japan made more of their shots and sealed the victory.

"I can't describe the sadness and disappointment we felt," Alex said, before adding, "We'd learn something from this, and we'd be back."

# CHAPTER 3
# 2012–2019

## STAR POWER

A year later, Team USA was back—at the 2012 London Olympics. Those who didn't know Alex Morgan before then certainly did after those games.

In recognition of her hard work and continuously improved play, Coach Sundhage had moved her from sub to starter. Alex soon proved the coach's confidence in her was well-deserved.

Two goals in the group stage win over France. An assist to Rapinoe in the win over Colombia. Another assist, this time to Wambach to beat North Korea. Another Morgan-to-Wambach assist in the 2–0 quarterfinal win over New Zealand.

And then, the semifinals versus Canada, a grueling, physical battle that was tied, 3–3, going into the final minutes of the second overtime.

"Who will face Japan in the final match? We have no idea!" an excited announcer cried over the roar of the fans.

At minute 123, they found out.

With forty-five seconds left on the clock, Team USA got control of the ball in Canada's half of the field. They closed in on the penalty box. Veteran Abby Wambach sent the ball to Heather O'Reilly on her far right.

Or meant to. The ball missed the target, forcing O'Reilly to chase after it. She controlled the ball close to the sideline and twisted around, looking for her teammates. Five Canadian defenders and keeper Erin McLeod stood between her and the goal. Wambach was there, too. So was Alex Morgan.

Alex had been a tireless force on offense all match, booting passes here, dribbling around defenders there, crashing the goal and assisting her teammates on near-misses. At minute 113, she was shoved hard to the ground and lay there for several seconds, before bounding up. O'Reilly saw her. Targeted her. And booted a high cross.

Had the pass gone to Wambach, chances were she would have headed it, her specialty. But headers were not Alex's favorite move, and McLeod seemed to know that. As the ball sailed through the air, she came off the line, ready to fend off a low shot.

But Alex surprised her. Instead of going low, she

went high, jumping above her defender and playing the ball off her head. Not the driving shot to a low corner McLeod seemed to be anticipating, but a high floater that arced over the defenders. Including McLeod.

"There was just that perfect gap in between her hands and the crossbar," Alex remembered. The ball threaded into the gap—and into the goal!

"At that moment, there was nothing else in my mind, but 'holy crap, that just went in!'" Alex recalled in an interview. She also remembered crying on the field as Wambach hugged her fiercely and said, "You just sent us to the gold-medal game."

Three days later, they won that gold-medal game, beating Japan 2–1 before a crowd of 80,000 fans in Wembley Stadium. It was their third consecutive Olympic championship, their fourth overall.

"Without a doubt," Alex said of the moment they put the gold medal around her neck, "the greatest achievement of my life."

Other achievements followed. In 2012, she signed a book deal to pen a series of middle-grade novels featuring the Kicks, a girls' soccer team; posed for a swimsuit photo shoot with *Sports Illustrated*; and best of all, was voted US Soccer Female Player of the Year. In early January 2013, she signed with the Portland Thorns, a team in the newly created National Women's Soccer League (NWSL). Later that year, she got engaged to her longtime boyfriend and fellow professional soccer player, Servando Carrasco, whom she married on December 31, 2014.

And of course, she trained and played with Team USA in preparation for the 2015 Women's World Cup. As much as she could, anyway. In the fall of 2013, Alex injured her ankle while playing for the Thorns. The injury was misdiagnosed as a sprain, and she returned to the field far sooner than she should have, aggravating the injury even more. She was out for seven months. She returned in time to take part in the 2014 CONCACAF qualifiers in October—only to reinjure the same ankle during the second group stage match.

"Having her go down is a big loss to the team," admitted Jill Ellis, Team USA's new head coach.

Then, just a few months after Alex returned to the field, she was injured again, this time with a bone bruise to her knee. Her teammates were optimistic that with rest and rehabilitation, she'd be ready for the 2015 World Cup in Canada.

And she was, although Coach Ellis kept her time to a minimum in the early matches. In the knockout round of sixteen, however, Alex showed she was more than ready to play. Minutes after the break in a scoreless game against Colombia—*wham!* She booted in the ball for the first goal of the game. Team USA ended up with the 2–0 win to stay alive.

They won their next games, too, thanks to Carli Lloyd's goal-scoring performances. By that time, Alex was playing nearly the whole game, and while she didn't contribute any goals, her efforts and enthusiasm helped boost the team. Alex nearly scored in the finals against their old nemesis, Japan, with a dangerous driving run. But it was Carli's hat trick in under sixteen minutes that stole the show and handed Team USA the win—their first World Cup title since 1999.

Alex was thrilled with the win. Later, though, she revealed she was disappointed in her own play and of how conscious she was of her nagging injuries. "I wasn't thinking about how to beat my opponent and be that fearless attacker," she said in an interview. "I was thinking about how to be pain-free."

Alex came roaring back for the 2016 Olympics in Brazil. She scored the second goal in the 2–0 win against New Zealand and Team USA's only goal in the quarterfinal match against Sweden.

That match ended in a tie in double overtime, forcing a penalty kick shoot-out. Alex was first up. She took careful aim, approached, kicked, and— *whap!* Sweden's keeper made the save. The game ended with Sweden winning on penalty kicks and the United States bowing out of the Olympics without reaching the semifinals for the first time in the team's history.

The crushing Olympic loss, "the toughest of her career," plus months of on-again, off-again pain took a toll on Alex emotionally. She felt her love for soccer starting to ebb. So in 2017, she made a bold move designed to recharge herself. She accepted an offer to play for Lyon, a professional team in France. She moved to Europe and poured herself into becoming the best player she could be. She made a move toward a healthier lifestyle, too, following a vegan diet and adding yoga and meditation to her exercise regimen.

The changes worked. By the end of August, she was back in the United States in top-notch form with the USWNT. How ready was she? "She's hungry," said Coach Ellis. "I mean this in the nicest way. She's a predator."

The hunger Coach Ellis saw in Alex Morgan came out in full force at the 2018 CONCACAF qualifiers. Team USA romped through the group stage, with Alex contributing two goals in two of the games. She added two more in the semifinals—and another in the finals for a grand total of seven! No one else scored as many, and Alex went home with the Golden Boot.

Those seven goals brought her USWNT total to ninety-seven. She made it ninety-eight during a friendly with Scotland in November 2018, and ninety-nine during another friendly, this time with Japan, at the end of February 2019. Number one hundred, a career milestone for any soccer player, came on April 4, 2019, in a friendly against Australia. She scored it in classic Alex Morgan style, on a fast break around a defender and a solid left-footed boot into the back of the net. Afterward, she saluted cheering fans by holding up her hands in a heart shape.

Fast-forward two months to June and the 2019 Women's World Cup in France. Team USA's first opponent in the group stage was Thailand. In what was later called "a simply stunning, ruthless, and clinical performance," the US players demolished the Thai 13–0. The score set a new World Cup record and had some people joking about the US women's team scoring more goals in one game than their male counterparts had in a season.

Five of those thirteen goals came from one player: Alex Morgan. She was awarded the Visa Player of the Match for her unbelievable scoring prowess. The award was handed to her by a surprise presenter—her mother!

Alex didn't score in the next few games, all victories for the United States. But in the semifinals against England—played on her thirtieth birthday—she dazzled her teammates and fans with a precision header in the thirty-first minute that gave Team USA the game-winning lead. She celebrated that goal with a controversial gesture, pretending to sip tea in an apparent taunt of England, where tea is a favorite beverage. She denied that she'd meant to disrespect their opponent, but many in the media were displeased.

Five days later, Alex and her teammates were back on the field for the finals against the Netherlands.

Before a crowd of nearly 58,000 cheering fans, the defending champions held off all attempts by the Dutch to score. But the Dutch defended their goal just as successfully and the score remained 0–0.

That's how it stayed until the sixtieth minute. Then Alex and the Netherlands' Stefanie van der Gragt made a play for the same high bouncing ball. Van der Gragt's leg flew up, and her cleat drove right into Alex's shoulder! The foul was missed on the field but caught by the video assistant referee. Since the foul occurred in the penalty box, the United States was awarded a penalty kick. Megan Rapinoe took it and, with one mighty blast, scored to put Team USA ahead by one. Then when Rose Lavelle, the team's fleet-footed midfielder, outraced a defender and booted the ball past the Dutch keeper, the United States took a 2–0 lead. When the Netherlands couldn't answer, Team USA was the world champion once again!

When asked to describe her emotions after the win, a tearful and ecstatic Alex Morgan, winner of the Silver Boot for her six goals, said, "I can't."

But a few days later, she found the words. She and her teammates were in Los Angeles to be part of the ESPYs, an award ceremony thrown by ESPN recognizing top athletic and team accomplishments. The USWNT received Best Team, and Alex was honored as Best Female Athlete.

During her acceptance speech, Alex glanced at the award with a smile and said, "Sorry, but this is probably the second-best trophy we won this week."

# ALEX MORGAN'S CAREER HIGHLIGHTS

## 2010

First US Women's National Team appearance, March 31

First US Women's National Team goal, October 6

## 2011

FIFA Women's World Cup: Silver Medal

## 2012

London Olympics: Gold Medal

US Soccer Female Player of the Year

## 2015

FIFA Women's World Cup: Gold Medal

ESPY Award: Best Team

## 2016

Played 100th cap, January 23

Rio Olympics: Fifth Place

## 2018

US Soccer Female Player of the Year

## 2019

Scored 100th career goal, April 4

Personal best record for greatest number of goals in a single game (5), June 11

FIFA Women's World Cup: Gold Medal

FIFA Women's World Cup: Silver Boot

ESPY Award: Best Female Athlete and Best Team

# MALLORY PUGH

Mallory Pugh goes for the ball while preparing for the 2019 Women's World Cup in a friendly match against Mexico.

Mallory Pugh scores a goal against Mexico leading up to the 2019 Women's World Cup.

# CHAPTER 1
# 1998–2011

## A STAR IN THE MAKING

Eighteen-year-old Mallory "Mal" Pugh was at a crossroads. She had recently started her freshman year at the University of California, Los Angeles. Thanks to a generous soccer scholarship, she had the opportunity to both get a top-notch education and gain valuable experience and exposure playing for a high-profile NCAA college team. Her life and her future looked to be on track.

There was just one problem: She wasn't happy.

"I'm comfortable," Mal remembered thinking. "I want to do something that makes me uncomfortable."

That "something" involved real-world experiences, like learning to live alone in her own apartment, managing her finances, and even buying groceries and preparing meals for herself. A life that took her to other countries, where she would interact with interesting people in different cultures. A life that revolved around playing soccer at the highest national and professional levels.

That life was well within her grasp. But it meant leaving UCLA. She knew that her soccer career would likely still be there for her after college. She knew, too, that it made sense to remain at UCLA, get her degree, and then pursue soccer. And yet...

"I just didn't feel right," Mallory said. "Not at UCLA, and not in general."

Those feelings persisted. After one semester, she was ready to make a choice between those two lives. She traveled home to Highlands Ranch, Colorado, during spring break to talk it over with her parents, Horace and Karen.

"She just said, 'You know what, I really feel this gut feeling. I want to go ahead and pursue the professional ranks,'" Horace remembered.

The Pughs understood their daughter's drive to move forward with her soccer career. Both parents came from athletic backgrounds themselves—Horace was a sprinter and long jumper and had played football in high school, and Karen was a long-distance runner. While her parents might have wished for Mal to stay in school, they recognized that she wouldn't be happy if she did.

"And so we said, 'Okay, we'll support you,'" Horace recalled.

Mallory's sister, Brianna, echoed their sentiment. Five-and-a-half years older than Mal, Bri had been a soccer standout on club teams, in high school, and at the University of Oregon. In 2014, she was called up to a training camp with the Under-23 Women's National Team.

But above all, Brianna was—and is—Mallory's best friend. "I can talk to her about anything," Mallory said.

When Mal told her she was thinking of pursuing a new dream, Brianna was encouraging. "She would always reference back to what I wanted to do when I was younger," Mallory remembered.

And what Mal wanted to do back then was play soccer. And practice soccer. And watch soccer. Basically, if it had anything to do with soccer, she wanted to be part of it!

Mallory Diane Pugh was born on April 29, 1998, in Littleton, Colorado. Her obsession with soccer began when she was around four years old. She had a thirteen-inch hot-pink Hello Kitty television in her bedroom. She didn't care that much about kids' programming, but if there was a soccer game being televised, she was glued to that set, even when the broadcast was in Spanish.

"I was just so desperate to watch soccer that I didn't care what TV it was on, or what language the call was in," Mallory said.

She watched live soccer, too, sitting in the bleachers while Brianna practiced and played with her club team, Real Colorado. "She would watch the whole game," recalled Jared Spires, Brianna's coach and later Mallory's as well. "And she loved to be around the team." He added that someone videoed Mallory joining the team when they ran around to acknowledge their parents.

"I was always looking up to her," Mallory said of her sister. "Everything she did, I wanted to do."

Brianna indulged Mallory's adoration—up to a point. When she and a friend kicked around a soccer ball in their backyard, they'd let Mal join in. Often, their play turned into a friendly match of two-on-one, with Brianna and her buddy going against the much younger, much smaller Mal! And sometimes Brianna would make her sister juggle the ball with her feet ten times before letting her back in the house.

Some little sisters might have dissolved into frustrated tears over such treatment. But not Mal. She thrived on the competition and enjoyed the challenge of trying to keep up with Brianna and her friends. "It was so unfair," she recalled with a laugh. "But it was so good for me."

All that watching and backyard practice paid off when Mallory was finally old enough to join a team of her own. She played recreational ball first, then followed in her sister's footsteps and tried out for Real Colorado. She made the team easily because her speed and technical ability were already greater than many of her peers'. It wasn't long before people took notice.

"She'll eat you alive," the coach of one rival team warned his players when they faced Real Colorado.

Part of Mallory's ferocity might stem from the fact that she has a very high pain threshold. As a child, she was always on the go and had more than her fair share of injuries. Most were minor, like bumps, bruises, and scrapes. But one was very serious. When she was twelve years old, her friends tried to hoist her up to her garage ceiling with a rope.

Mallory thought it was funny—until she fell and broke her wrist. When Horace told her she'd have to miss the upcoming tournament that weekend, Mal took hold of the twisted bones and wrenched them back in place—and then played the whole tournament with her wrist wrapped in bubble wrap!

"I think she scored, like, eight goals," Coach Spires said.

With her combination of speed, fearlessness, and talent for sending the ball into the back of the net, Mallory helped her U-12 Real Colorado team win the state championship in 2010 and her U-13 team take the same title in 2011. "Girls would have no chance," a player from a team that faced Mallory and Real Colorado recalled in an interview. "The amount of goals she scored was unreal in our club days."

Mallory's successes on the field fueled her passion for soccer. She felt she was ready for greater challenges. And that summer, the perfect opportunity came her way.

# CHAPTER 2
# 2011–2016

## ON HER WAY UP...AND UP...AND UP!

Horace and Denise Pugh believed their younger daughter brought something special to the soccer field. They wanted to support her dream of advancing to higher levels of play. So when Mallory received an invitation to the US Soccer U-14 training camp in Portland, Oregon, in the summer of 2011, they didn't hesitate to send her.

The purpose of the camp was to identify potential future players for Team USA. Mallory traveled by plane to the camp alone. There, she found herself surrounded by the region's top talent in her age group, most of them older, bigger, and stronger. "I thought the girls around me were so much better," she remembered.

The evaluators—including one very important coach: Jill Ellis, the future leader of the USWNT—disagreed. Jill made sure Mallory was invited back to a second camp a few weeks later, and then kept her eye on the speedy youngster with the fierce attacking skills in the next seasons.

Such attention fanned the fire of Mal's obsession with soccer. By then, she was already imagining herself playing on the world stage. "I want to be on the USA soccer team and win a gold medal!" proclaims the quote beside her sixth-grade yearbook picture.

With people like Jill Ellis following her fledgling career, Mallory was on her way to achieving that dream. But in early fall of 2012, just after she entered Mountain Vista High School, she suffered an injury that could have ended her career before it began. She was playing a match with Real Colorado when a player on the other team tackled her. Tackles are part of the game, and this one wasn't particularly nasty. But Mallory's leg bent awkwardly. Her femur, the leg's biggest bone, snapped. And just like that, she was sidelined for seven months. Luckily, the break healed in time for her to try out for the high school soccer team. Her skills hadn't deteriorated at all during her time off the field, and she made the varsity team. That season, she played in fourteen games, scored ten goals, and helped the Golden Eagles to a record of 19–1 and a Class 5A state title. The following two years, she took part in just eighteen games total but booted in an average of two goals and one assist per game! She received numerous awards, including MaxPreps Player of the Game, MaxPreps All-State First Team, and Gatorade National Girls Soccer Player of the Year.

Mallory was on the team roster her senior year, too. But while she attended practices and was on the sidelines in uniform during every game in 2016, she didn't play. Not because her skills had fallen off or because she was injured, but because she was making her mark on the international soccer stage instead.

Rewind to 2013. In January, fourteen-year-old Mallory was invited to train with the US U-15 Girls' National Team, a squad for outstanding players under the age of fifteen. She performed so well there that she received more invitations to other camps later in the year. But not for the U-15 team—for the U-17 Women's National Team! She impressed the evaluators and coaches so much that they named her to the roster that fall. It was a huge achievement for Mal, who was just fifteen.

In late October 2013, she traveled with the squad to Jamaica for the U-17 Confederation of North,

Central American, and Caribbean Association Football (CONCACAF) qualifiers. It was an important tournament because the teams that came out in first and second place would advance to the U-17 Women's World Cup the following year.

Team USA played their first game on Halloween against Trinidad and Tobago. In the thirty-first minute, Mallory scored her first goal as a member of the national team—and her second late in the second half! A third goal came a few days later in a match against Canada. The United States looked poised to be in the finals. But they fell to Mexico in the semifinals in a game decided on penalty kicks. They finished in third place overall, with Mallory drilling in two more goals for a tournament total of five—six, including a penalty kick in the disappointing loss to Mexico. Sadly, a third-place finish wasn't enough to get the team to the 2014 U-17 Women's World Cup.

Mallory did participate in a World Cup in 2014, though—as a member of the U-20 Women's National Team!

In February 2014, the fifteen-year-old standout was called up to the older-age training camp. It was a huge honor, and a promising step forward in her young career, for the U-20 team served as a feeder for the United States Women's National Team (USWNT). If she made the U-20 roster, she had a better chance of someday being invited to try out for Team USA, the best squad in the nation!

Mallory performed well enough at the February session to get a second look at the April camp. And then two more camps in May and June. When the roster for the 2014 U-20 Women's World Cup was announced in July, her name was on it.

At just sixteen years old, she was the youngest player on the team. Her technical skills, confidence, and heads-up play impressed the older players, including fellow Colorado native and future member of the USWNT Lindsey Horan. Horan had heard about the phenom from her home state, but being four years older, she hadn't seen Mallory play until the February training camp. She was struck by the teenager's ability on the field as well as the mature way she handled herself off the field.

"It really isn't like she's sixteen years old," Horan said.

While Mallory didn't score during the August 2014 World Cup tournament, she saw plenty of playing time. She even returned to the field after suffering an ankle injury, drawing on her ability to ignore pain to come off the sidelines. Unfortunately, the United States fell short of the finals, coming in fourth overall.

It was a different story in December 2015, however. Earlier that year, Mallory had celebrated with US soccer fans when the USWNT won the Women's World Cup in Vancouver. She and her U-20 teammates rode that wave of energy into the CONCACAF qualifiers in Honduras. In the team's first match, against Mexico, the United States was awarded a penalty kick after a Mexican player committed a handball foul inside the box. Mallory took the kick—and blasted a beauty right under the crossbar and out of the keeper's reach!

Three days later, she added two more goals in the 6–1 win over Panama, then two more in a 6–0 victory over Haiti. And she wasn't done yet. In the semifinals with Honduras—*pow!*—Mal sent the ball into the net off a pass following a corner kick to give Team USA a 2–0 lead. She helped widen the gap twenty-five minutes later, outdistancing her defender and belting in a goal from seventeen yards out. Team USA won the game 7–0.

Seven was also the total number of goals Mal herself put in by the end of the tournament, the most of any player. She was awarded the Golden Boot for most goals scored as well as the Golden Ball for best overall player. She was also named US Soccer Young Female Player of the Year. Thanks in large part to her outstanding heads-up play and energy, Team USA emerged as the CONCACAF champions. They would play in the 2016 U-20 World Cup.

But Mallory wouldn't be going with them.

Not long after her blistering performance in Honduras, she received an exciting call from US Soccer. They wanted her on the USWNT roster. Not the U-17 or U-20 teams. *The* USWNT. Starting immediately.

The seventeen-year-old joined her new teammates in January 2016. She was beside herself with excitement but also very nervous. The World Cup–winning team was stacked with the greatest names in women's soccer—veterans like Carli Lloyd, Tobin Heath, Hope Solo, Megan Rapinoe, and others—some of whom were ten or more years older than Mallory. "I was like, 'What am I doing?'" she said. "'I'm playing next to *Tobin*. I'm playing next to *Pinoe*. I'm playing next to *Carli*. What is happening?'"

Those players trained and played harder than

anyone she'd ever been on a team with. And they expected her to do the same.

"Not treating her like a young player" is how teammate Crystal Dunn described the way they brought Mal into the fold, and instead "treating her like she's any player on the team."

That treatment included good-natured jibes aimed at her youth. "They'd just joke like, 'Oh, Mal, you got prom?'" Mallory remembered with a smile. Her older teammates liked to point out that she'd been only fifteen months old when the now-legendary players on the 1999 USWNT—Mia Hamm, Michelle Akers, Kristine Lilly, among others—had taken home their first World Cup.

Mallory rolled with the jokes off the field. And on the field, she showed everyone why she'd been put on the roster despite still being in high school. With a combination of speed, aggression, and tenacity, she cut around and burst through defenses on the way to the goal. When a teammate reminded her that defense was equally important as offense, Mal worked hard to improve that part of her game.

But what most impressed her teammates right from the start was her attitude. Despite her meteoric rise to the top of the soccer world, she showed no arrogance, but rather a refreshing humility and quiet confidence. She didn't crave the spotlight the way some newly famous seventeen-year-olds might have. Just the opposite—she wished all the attention would go away.

"I would rather go out in the field and play," she told a reporter once.

She did just that on January 23, 2016, her debut game—known as a cap in soccer lingo—with Team USA. The match was a friendly—a scrimmage, or practice game, that doesn't count in either team's rankings—with Ireland played in San Diego, California. She'd already set a record just by stepping onto the field in the fifty-eighth minute, the youngest player since 2002 to do so. Then, seconds before the eighty-third minute, she made history again.

Team USA was well on their way to defeating Ireland, having built a comfortable 4–0 lead. They didn't let up, though. Instead, they went on the attack, bringing the ball down the left side of the field. Deep into Ireland's territory, US striker Christen Press moved to collect a pass inside the box. The ball was nudged away by an Irish defender. Press chased it to the goal line, controlled it, and spun around to send a cross in front of the goal.

Like a shot, Mallory darted in and—*pow!*—zinged a header past the keeper and into the goal!

"And what a finish!" an announcer enthused as Press wrapped a joyful Mal into a bear hug and lifted her off the ground. More teammates swarmed the pair, slapping Mal on the back and joining Press for a group hug. With that goal, Mal became the youngest USWNT player to score in her first cap.

Her second USWNT goal came less than a month before her eighteenth birthday, on April 6. It was during another friendly, this time against Colombia in Hartford, Connecticut. Team USA had the ball inside the circle in front of Colombia's goal. Carli Lloyd and Tobin Heath flicked the ball back and forth, evading defenders and looking for an opportunity to score.

Meanwhile, Mallory sneaked in from the left. Lloyd saw her. She twisted around, creating enough space to get off a pass, and delivered a pinpoint shot to her young teammate. Mal took two quick touches, then drilled the ball into the net.

"At such a young age, Mallory Pugh has the class to look up and finish it right where she needs to," an announcer said admiringly. "Right over the goalkeeper's leg."

Mallory, now eighteen, added a third, unassisted goal at the end of July. That night, one of the greatest soccer players of all time commented on her play. "Speed kills, but technical skill absolutely annihilates defenders," two-time Olympic gold medalist and World Cup winner Mia Hamm posted on social media. "Mallory Pugh is for real."

That praise from a player Mallory considered a hero was an enormous confidence booster. And it couldn't have come at a better time—a few weeks later, Team USA would head to Rio de Janeiro for the 2016 Olympics.

Mallory tried to pretend she wasn't fazed by the prospect of taking the field for some of the highest-profile matches of the decade. But still..."Being able to say that you're an Olympian?" she commented before boarding the plane. "That's crazy."

Team USA got off to a strong start with a 2–0 win over New Zealand, followed by a too-close-for-comfort 1–0 victory over France. Their final match in the group stage was against Colombia. Colombia got on the board first with a slow-rolling free kick, known as a "howler," from Catalina Usme that somehow made it through keeper Hope Solo's outstretched hands. Usme got in the record books as the player who scored her country's first-ever Olympic goal.

Team USA tied it in the forty-first minute when Crystal Dunn caught a ricochet off the crossbar and booted the ball over the goal line. Dunn was instrumental in the team's second goal, too. This time, she raced down the left sideline with the ball, then fired off a pass toward the net. Two US players went for the ball. After a momentary tangle-up, one emerged with it, tapped it twice, then drilled a left-footer past two defenders and the Colombian keeper for a goal.

That player? Mallory Pugh, making her the youngest US player to score a goal in the Olympics.

"It kind of felt like any other goal," she admitted later before adding that scoring in the Olympics was "actually pretty cool."

Had the United States held on to their 2–1 lead for the rest of the game, that goal might have felt even better. But they didn't. In the ninetieth minute, Usme struck again with another free kick that Solo couldn't get her hands on. The game ended in a draw.

Next up was the quarterfinals against Sweden, another hard-fought, low-scoring match that saw

Team USA tying it up 1–1 in the seventy-seventh minute with a beautiful goal from Alex Morgan. The game remained tied at the end of regulation time. And was still tied after two fifteen-minute overtime periods. The winners, and the team that would advance to the semifinals, would be determined by a penalty kick shoot-out.

Five players from each team took turns kicking. After both were through, one team had scored more goals than the other. That team was Sweden. For the first time in sixteen years, Team USA had failed to advance past the quarterfinals.

It was a bitter blow to the players and their fans. But they couldn't dwell on it for too long. They had to start preparing for the next big tournament, the 2019 Women's World Cup.

Mal had some preparing to do, too—for college life at UCLA. But already, she was questioning whether that was the right move for her. And then came her April 17, 2017, announcement that she had chosen to withdraw from the school to pursue her professional soccer career.

"This decision was certainly not easy for me to make," Mallory said.

Her choice to leave college saw mixed reactions

from the public. While some thought it was a mistake to leave school, others believed she was doing the right thing in pursuing her professional athletic goals.

"I think it's fantastic," USWNT coach Jill Ellis said. "We have to get to a point in this country where our top players are seeking out the most challenging environments."

And with her tough decision behind her, Mallory couldn't wait to dive right into that environment.

# CHAPTER 3
# 2017–2019

## OLYMPIAN AND WORLD CHAMP

At nineteen, Mallory Pugh had had more life experiences than many people much older. In the spring of 2017, she added one more: moving across the country and living on her own. She found an apartment in Washington, DC, and joined her new National Women's Soccer League (NWSL) team, the Washington Spirit, in early May. She played in her first match on May 20, 2017. She got her first start eight days later and made her first goal the following game. Five more goals followed, giving her a season total of six in sixteen games. Her outstanding play put her in the running for NWSL's Rookie of the Year award, and while she didn't garner that award—it went to her future Spirit teammate Ashley Hatch—Mallory was happy with how her first season went.

And just because she was on the Spirit didn't mean she had to give up her spot on Team USA.

Players on both the USWNT and NWSL rosters were granted time away to train with and play for the national team, and Mallory made the most of every experience with that elite squad. In a mid-September friendly, her twenty-eighth cap, she scored her sixth career goal. More surely would have followed that fall if not for a disastrous moment a month later.

Team USA was playing a friendly against South Korea on October 19. They were up 2–0 heading toward the halftime break. In the forty-fourth minute, Mallory challenged a South Korean with a hard tackle. The South Korean player went down. The ball rolled free and in Mal's direction. But she didn't go for it...because she was hopping awkwardly on her left leg. And then she dropped to the ground, clutching the back of her right leg and choking on tears of pain. Play stopped as her concerned teammates hurried to her side. The trainers ran on and helped her to her feet. She tried to put weight on the leg and immediately collapsed. They ended up carrying her off the field.

Diagnosis: a bad hamstring pull.

Mallory sat out the rest of 2017 but returned in full force at the start of 2018. Her second game back with Team USA, she ripped off two unassisted goals in the 5–1 win over Denmark. Three more goals followed in March and April.

But then injury struck again in late May. Mal was back with the Spirit, playing in a game in Houston, when during an aggressive attack she collided with the Houston Dash's goalkeeper. She wrenched her knee badly. She didn't need surgery, but she was sidelined for several weeks.

She overcame her injury and was back in uniform for Team USA for the 2018 CONCACAF qualifiers in October. But for the first time in her career, Mallory found herself spending more time on the bench than on the field. The time away from the game while she was healing had taken its toll on her level of play. While she was undoubtedly still one of the top players in the United States with years of stellar performances ahead of her, others on the team were simply one step ahead of her at the moment.

She was dismayed to watch so many of the matches from the sidelines. But she refused to spiral down too far emotionally. Instead, she drew on her own inner strength to bolster her spirits. "I just have to remind myself, 'Yeah, you're good enough. You're here for a reason.'"

Her teammates were quick to reassure her, too, both in person and on the record to interviewers. "It's a challenging environment," pointed out Megan Rapinoe. "[But] she just gets it. She sees the bigger picture."

"You give Mal space," agreed Alex Morgan, "and she'll do magic with it."

Team USA won the 2018 CONCACAF qualifiers to earn a berth in the 2019 Women's World Cup in France. For Mallory, the qualifiers had been a wake-up call. As good as she was, there was always room for improvement. She returned home knowing two things: her place on the World Cup roster was by no means guaranteed and getting on that roster was the single most important goal of her life.

So she got down to work, training and playing hard to prove that she belonged. "I go out every single day and try to be better than I was the previous day," she said in an interview. "I know by making those one percent gains, I will hopefully make the team."

She learned that her hard work and dedication had paid off right before training camps. She was in her apartment in Washington when her phone rang. Coach Ellis was on the other line. It was a make-or-break moment for Mallory—had she done enough to make the team, or would she be watching the 2019 Women's World Cup on television at home?

Coach Ellis didn't keep her in suspense. Mallory had made the roster!

Knowing she was on the team was a huge relief. But it also meant "it was time to take it into the next gear," Mal remembered thinking.

Working alongside her teammates definitely helped. "I realized I am learning from the best forwards in the world," she said. "They're passionate and great role models. To be in that environment every single day made me better."

When the 2019 Women's World Cup opened in France on June 7, Mallory felt more than ready to do her part to help the team defend its 2015 title.

Team USA got off to a rollicking start with a 13–0 victory over Thailand, thanks in large part to Alex Morgan's record-tying five goals. Mal contributed to the total, too, coming off the bench in the sixty-ninth minute and netting the team's eleventh goal in the eighty-fifth minute. It wasn't an important goal in the runaway game—but it meant a lot to Mallory. It was her first World Cup goal, and it gave her a much-needed jolt of confidence.

That goal would be the only one she made in the three games she played, however. While she was playing well, other, more experienced members of the team were playing better. Coach Ellis believed Mallory was a strong player and, at just twenty-one years old, one who had a bright future ahead of her. But this was the World Cup, the premier women's soccer sporting event. The coach needed to field her best eleven players if Team USA was to repeat as world champs. And she needed talented substitutes ready to go in at a moment's notice if necessary.

That moment didn't arrive for Mallory. But she was one of the loudest voices on the bench, cheering madly as Megan Rapinoe booted two penalty kicks into the net for Team USA's 2–1 victory over Spain in the knockout round. Her shouts were equally loud and joyful when Rapinoe scored both goals in the 2–1 win over France in the quarterfinals and the 2–1 victory in the semifinals against England with goals from Alex Morgan and Christen Press. And she was absolutely over the moon when her friend, teammate, and Washington, DC, room-mate, Rose Lavelle, sneaked in under the radar and scored the winning goal in the finals to give the defending World Cup champions their second con-secutive title.

"It's inspiring for me," Mal said of Lavelle in the press conference after the Cup, "and it makes me want to be better." Then she added, "She *rose* to the occasion!"—and burst out laughing when she realized she'd made a pun with her friend's name.

Of course, Mallory would have loved to have been the one to score that winning goal, or any of the others that led to Team USA's World Cup tri-umph. But she wasn't discouraged not to have seen more playing time. Just the opposite, in fact.

"I've never been so motivated in my life," she said. "I now know the work required to put in, but I also know there's so much more that has to happen. I just have to keep pushing."

Pushing has never been a problem for the young woman who went against the norm and chose a dif-ferent, less comfortable path for herself. Nowadays, when she's not on the field, she's busy with vari-ous endorsement deals, including commercials for

Gatorade. In one ad, she actually shares the screen with her idol, Mia Hamm!

But mostly, she's devoting her time to the sport she's been obsessed with since she was four years old. For even though she has achieved her sixth-grade dream of playing for Team USA and winning a gold medal—earning worldwide recognition—the twenty-one-year-old dynamo is nowhere near ready to step away from the field.

In fact, two weeks after celebrating with parades, talk show appearances, and awards parties back home in the United States, Mallory got right back on the field in her NWSL Spirit uniform, battling every minute she played to get her foot on the ball and score. At the start of 2020, she'll rejoin her USWNT teammates for training camps and friend-lies. And she'll play every game, train every day, with her eye focused on Team USA's next big challenge: the 2020 Summer Olympics in Tokyo.

Through it all, she'll have the support of those who have been with her right from the start: Horace, Denise, and Brianna. "We joke about it now," Brianna once said. "We're like, 'Great, we taught her everything we know, and she's this super-star now.'"

A superstar, yes, and a player teammates and fans hope will have a long, storied career. And if that career involves scoring goals, that'll be just fine with Mallory Pugh. Because as she once said, "I just like scoring goals. And once you can do it? You're like, 'Ooh, I shouldn't stop!'"

# MALLORY PUGH'S CAREER HIGHLIGHTS

## 2015

US Soccer Young Female Player of the Year

## 2016

First US Women's National Team appearance,
January 23

First US Women's National Team goal,
January 23

Rio Olympics: Fifth Place

## 2019

FIFA Women's World Cup: Gold Medal

ESPY Award: Best Team

# M GAN RAPI OE

Megan Rapinoe fights for the ball during a Tournament of Nations game on July 29, 2018, against Australia. The game ended in a draw, 1–1.

Megan Rapinoe hoists the Golden Ball above her head after the US team's victory over the Netherlands in the 2019 Women's World Cup final.

# CHAPTER 1
# 1985–2006

## FROM REDDING TO READY

The atmosphere in the United States Women's National Team (USWNT) locker room at halftime was serious. Businesslike, even. Players discussed why they'd missed opportunities to score and encouraged one another to play harder, run faster, and keep up the pressure on their Japanese opponents. They talked about strategies and plays, Japan's weaknesses and strengths. Anyone listening to them would have thought they were deep in the hole.

In fact, they were ahead 4–1 in the final game of the 2015 Women's World Cup. Amazingly, all four of Team USA's goals had been scored in the first sixteen minutes of the game—and even more amazingly, three of them were made by one player, Carli Lloyd, a first in World Cup history.

And yet no one seemed excited.

Midfielder Megan "Pinoe" Rapinoe was, though— very, very excited. She had been holding her emotions in check. But finally, she just couldn't take it anymore. She jumped to her feet and burst out, "We're gonna win the World Cup!"

An impish grin split her face as she repeated those words. "WE'RE. GONNA. WIN. THE. WORLD CUP!"

Pinoe's enthusiasm was infectious. When the second half started, her teammates rode that wave of excitement back onto the field. Forty-five minutes later, they did exactly what she'd predicted.

They won the World Cup.

Megan Anna Rapinoe's journey to the 2015 World Cup championship began in Redding, California, where she was born on July 5, 1985. She is the youngest child of Denise and Jim Rapinoe, but not by much. Rachael, her fraternal twin sister, was born just eleven minutes earlier. They joined four other siblings, CeCe, Jennifer, Michael, and Brian, in the Rapinoe household. The older three were nearly out of the house by the time the Rapinoe twins arrived, but five-year-old Brian was still present. And in Megan's world, he was a *presence*.

"I worshipped him," she remembered once. As toddlers, she and Rachael watched Brian's soccer games from the sidelines. When they were four and he was nine, he started teaching them how to play. He took them to the churchyard across the street from their house, set up cones, and showed them how to dribble, shoot, and pass. Megan couldn't wait to play on her own team, and when she did, she wanted to be just like him.

"He played left wing, so I played left wing," she said once. "He wore No. 7; I wore No. 7. He got a bowl [hair]cut, so I did, too."

Megan's love for her older brother was tested more than once growing up. Brian began using drugs when he was twelve, was arrested and sent to juvenile detention when he was fifteen, and was in and out of jail for many years afterward. His choices and behavior left Megan feeling very confused, hurt, and angry. Yet she never let his addiction and troubles with the law uproot her love for him. To this day, she remains fiercely loyal to her brother.

But the person who had the greatest influence in her life was Rachael. "She's my other half in this world," Megan once said. The two were insepar-able as children. They went to school together and shared a bedroom. They built tree forts and fished for crawdads in the nearby creek, using bacon sneaked out of the refrigerator as bait. They played house and one-on-one baseball.

Like many siblings, they bickered constantly—about Megan's messy side of the room, whether a ball had been hit fair or foul, and many other things. Playtime ended and arguments were quickly forgotten, though, when their mother summoned them home with ear-piercing whistles made by putting her pinkies in her mouth. When the twins heard those whistles, they knew they had to hustle. "If you weren't home in the next ten or fifteen minutes, you were in trouble," Megan said.

Megan was always on the go as a child—except in gym class at Junction Avenue K–8 Elementary School, where her lack of effort earned her Bs instead of the As one might expect from someone who loved sports so much. "I wasn't going to get all sweaty!" she recalled with a laugh.

As she and Rachael grew older, they spent more of their free time playing sports with their classmates, both boys and girls. "We used to go from playing street hockey in full gear, to playing basketball, then break for lunch, then play some soccer, then back into the street hockey gear," Megan remembered.

They did organized sports, too—track and field

in middle school and high school, as well as basketball. Megan's competitiveness kicked into high gear on the court, though perhaps a bit too high. "I fouled out of almost every basketball game in high school," she once admitted.

And of course, Megan and Rachael played soccer. In elementary and middle school, their teams, the Under-12 and Under-14 Mavericks, were coached by their father, Jim. Both girls were standouts on the field and all but assured starting positions on the Foothill High School roster.

But they never played for the school team. Instead, they joined Elk Grove Pride (later United), a high-profile club team. The coach, Danny Cruz, had seen the twins play in middle school when Elk Grove faced off against the Mavericks in Redding. "I have to get these players on my team," he remembered thinking. "They are phenomenal."

Cruz was right: They were phenomenal, especially Megan. Thanks to Brian, she'd always been interested in soccer. That interest spiked on July 4, 1999. Megan and Rachael were at Stanford Stadium for the semifinals of the Women's World Cup. Seeing Mia Hamm, Briana Scurry, Julie Foudy, and her personal hero, Kristine Lilly, play before a crowd of

73,000 screaming fans, watching them beat Brazil, knowing they were on their way to the final match, was "one of the more transformative experiences of my life," Megan said.

She was already a very good player. As a middle schooler, she had made the U-14 Olympic Development Program. In 2002, she was on the roster for the U-16 Girls' National Team. She was honored to be part of these teams, of course, and she learned a great deal from playing with those high-caliber players and coaches. But those training camps and tournaments didn't happen all the time. To keep up her level of play, she needed regular practices and games with challenging competition. So when Coach Cruz contacted her, she jumped at the chance to play for Elk Grove. So did Rachael, who loved soccer just as much as her twin.

There was just one problem: The club was a two-and-a-half-hour drive from Redding! But even then, Denise and Jim understood their daughters were something special on the field. If they played for Elk Grove, they'd get much more exposure than if they played for Foothill High. So, starting in 2002 and for the next few years, they made the three-hundred-mile trek to weekly practices and weekend tournaments.

With the Rapinoe sisters on the roster, Elk Grove won the state and regional championships in 2003. A tying goal by Megan in the national game almost netted them the national title that year as well. But their opponents, the Peachtree City Lazers, took the lead late in the game and won, 2–1.

Megan stayed on the Elk Grove roster through 2005, but she didn't play many games for them. That's because she was busy with two new teams. One was the Pilots, the team at the University of Portland, where both she and Rachael had chosen to go after graduating from high school in 2004. The UP Pilots had a strong soccer program that boasted Olympians and World Cup winners Shannon MacMillan and Tiffeny Milbrett as alumni. It was definitely the right place for both Rapinoe girls.

But only Rachael started at UP in the fall of 2004. Megan redshirted, meaning she chose to put off enrolling and playing for one year. That's because she needed to train and travel with her second soccer team: the U-19 Women's National Team.

Megan had made the squad after attending a training camp in California in January 2003. Called a "slick forward...with a nose for the goal" in a players' roundup by US Soccer, she practiced with the team off and on that winter and spring. In late May, she traveled with them to Houston for the United States Youth Soccer Cup. There, she scored her first goal for the team—in the very first minute of the first match! Later that summer, she also got her first real taste of playing overseas in a U-19 tournament held in Europe.

She made the U-19 roster again in 2004 and, in late May, journeyed with the team to Ottawa for the Confederation of North, Central American, and Caribbean Association Football (CONCACAF) U-19 qualifiers. Team USA romped past the Dominican Republic in their first match, 14–0, with Megan contributing two goals. She added a third in their win over Trinidad and Tobago.

The United States fell to Canada in the finals, but their second-place win earned them a berth in the 2004 U-19 Women's World Cup in Thailand.

Team USA won their first game on November 11 against South Korea. Three days later, they won again, 4–1 over Russia, with Megan contributing one of those goals. The U-19s then beat Spain, 1–0, to advance to the quarterfinals.

Megan lit up the field in that match against Australia. She came close to giving Team USA an early lead with a near-miss header off a corner kick. She followed that with a sharp shot from twenty-two yards out that skimmed the outside of the left post, and then another powerful blast from twenty yards that the Australian keeper dove for and saved. But the keeper couldn't stop Megan's teammate Amy Rodriguez from scoring early in the second half, or the long, curving ball Megan kicked in the second half. Final score: USA 2, Australia 0.

While Team USA lost 3–1 to Germany in the semifinal round, they took home the bronze by beating Brazil 3–0. Megan scored one of those goals, giving her a tournament total of three, plus one assist, in the five games she played.

By the end of 2004, soccer watchers were taking note of the nineteen-year-old with the aggressive, creative style of play, who charged fearlessly toward and around defenders and carved out scoring opportunities where none seemed to exist. One of those people was Jill Ellis, coach of the U-21 team. At the start of 2005, she called Megan up to the squad.

That kicked off a whirlwind year of soccer for Megan. She attended three weeklong U-21 training camps in the first half of the year. In late July, she traveled to Sweden to play in the Nordic Cup. One month later, she joined Rachael at the University of

Portland to play in her first season with the Pilots. She started in all twenty-five college games, scored fifteen goals—seven of them game winners—and assisted on thirteen others to help the Pilots to an outstanding 23–0–2 season record and the team's first NCAA title. She ended 2005 receiving several awards, including *Soccer Times* National Freshman of the Year, West Coast Conference Freshman of the Year, and the NCAA All-Tournament Team.

And her crazy soccer schedule didn't stop there. A few weeks after the Pilots' season ended, Megan reported to the January training camp for the national team. Not the U-21 squad—the senior USWNT! Her aggressive style of play, skilled footwork, and ability to read the field earned her a spot on the 2006 roster along with stars Abby Wambach, Kristine Lilly, Christie Rampone, and up-and-comer Carli Lloyd.

One of the first people she saw at that camp, though, was a hero of hers. "Kristine walked into the room," Megan said, "[and] I was sitting there like, 'Oh my God, oh my God, what do I say, what do I do, who am I, what's happening?'"

Lilly's down-to-earth demeanor made a huge impression on Megan. She understood then that you could be a star and still be a decent human being, too.

Megan—or Pinoe, as her friends and teammates called her—trained hard with the team in the following months. On July 23, 2006, she got her first cap—the soccer term for a game played with the national team—in a game against Ireland. Sandy hair tied back in a messy bun, she trotted onto the field just before the sixty-ninth minute. With the score USA 3, Ireland 0, the game looked to be in the bag. So Pinoe had one objective in mind: "Not to royally mess up!"

Her first USWNT goal came on October 1 in a game against China. The match was already an 8–0 runaway for Team USA. Yet when Pinoe drilled in number nine for the team, she was thrilled. She didn't show it, though, except for a huge smile. Instead, she reminded herself not to celebrate, just to get ready for the next kickoff. It was a reminder she had to repeat when she scored a second goal that same game!

Just a few days after that match, Pinoe was back on the field for the Portland Pilots. She was playing better than she ever had and was starting to dream about a future playing soccer professionally.

But on October 5, 2006, that future came crashing down.

# CHAPTER 2
# 2006–2011

## DOWN, BUT NOT OUT

A pop. That's the sound Pinoe's left knee made when she slipped and fell on the turf during the October 5 game against Washington State. For a split second, nothing changed. Then the pain hit— and she knew.

She'd torn her ACL, a major ligament in her knee. "It's a feeling like nothing else," she recalled. "My first thoughts were 'Oh my gosh. This can't be happening.'"

ACL tears have ended many athletes' careers. But Pinoe refused to let that happen. After surgery to repair the damage, she threw herself into rehab. By the summer of 2007, she was back on the field. But not on the USWNT roster. After being out for months, she'd lost her slot in the lineup.

That September, she was back home instead of in China with Team USA for the 2007 Women's World Cup. To make matters even worse, she watched that

World Cup while recovering from a *second* ACL injury to the same knee. "I tried to be that super athlete who can bounce right back," she admitted. She'd tweaked the knee during a late August practice with the Pilots. Rather than have it evaluated, she ignored the pain and hoped for the best.

She got the worst. Ten minutes into a game on September 14, she came out limping. A second surgery on September 25 dealt with the tear. And then came more long months of rehab.

This time, she had a rehab partner—Rachael. Eerily, her twin had torn her own ACL just one week before Megan. "It's almost stupid that this is happening," she told a reporter. "Now we're going through the same thing at the same time. So hopefully we get back at the same point." Rachael recovered to play again for the Pilots in 2008, but a second injury to that same knee eventually ended her soccer career.

That could have been Pinoe's fate, too, had her second tear been worse. Or if she had allowed the setback to plunge her into despair, as it would have many other athletes. Instead, she focused on the process of healing. It wasn't easy. The USWNT was scheduled to play in the 2008 Beijing Olympics in

August, and every fiber of her being wanted to hurry through rehab so she could regain her slot in the lineup.

But she didn't, and in the long run, her patience was worth it. Against all odds, she emerged from rehab physically and emotionally stronger than after her first ACL injury. More important, the time off the field made her realize how much she wanted to be *on* the field—as a professional soccer player. "I really appreciate everything more in terms of my soccer life," she once said, "because I know what it's like to have it all taken away, two times in a row."

On August 23, two days after Team USA won the Olympic gold medal, and following months of rehab, Pinoe got back into the game as a starter for the Portland Pilots. By the end of the 2008 UP season, she had drilled in four goals, ten assists, and been named the West Coast Conference Player of the Year. With her in the lineup, the Pilots reached the quarterfinals of the NCAA tournament. It was an amazing comeback after two years riddled with injuries, surgeries, and rehab.

And it wasn't the only comeback she had that year. In early December, Pinoe was home for the holidays when the phone rang. On the other end was Pia Sundhage, coach of the USWNT. She had an important question for Megan: "Are you fit?"

Pinoe's answer? A resounding, heartfelt YES!

Sundhage invited Megan to the January 2009 training camp. Pinoe shone during that week. She made the roster and, on March 4, came off the bench during the Algarve Cup to play in her first match. She played well enough to earn starts in the next two games.

Their opponent in that third match was Norway, always a tough team. But Team USA was tough, too. In the twenty-first minute, Kacey White dribbled the ball down the sideline. She booted a pass to Amy Rodriguez at the top of Norway's penalty box. Rodriguez spun around and found Pinoe near the goal. Pinoe evaded Norway's defenders with a few quick touches, then *wham!* She slammed a shot across the goal. The ball struck the left post and ricocheted into the net!

That was the only goal Team USA scored that game. But it was all they needed. Final score: USA 1, Norway 0. Pinoe helped the team beat Sweden in the championship game two days later, booting an assist to Shannon Boxx that tied the score 1–1 in the final seconds. Though the United States lost in a penalty kick shootout, the team wouldn't have reached that point without Pinoe.

She continued her strong play for the remainder of 2009. To no one's surprise, she was on the roster again in 2010. Number one priority for her and her teammates that year? Earn a berth in the 2011 Women's World Cup by coming in first or second at the 2010 CONCACAF qualifiers in late October.

Unfortunately, Pinoe was struck down by a stomach illness that kept her from participating in the January training camp. She didn't make it off the bench at the Algarve Cup in early March, and she wasn't even on the roster in two friendlies later that same month.

She finally made it back into the action in late May as a sub and then at long last as a starter in a friendly against Sweden on July 13. After that, she didn't look back. July 17—*boom!* She scored her first goal of the season in a 3–0 win over Sweden. October 2, she scored again, helping Team USA to a 2–1 victory over China.

Next stop: the CONCACAF qualifiers in Cancún, Mexico. The United States chalked up a solid 5–0 win over Haiti in their first group stage match. Two days later, Pinoe contributed two goals in the team's

9–0 victory over Guatemala. When Team USA won their last group stage match 4–0 over Costa Rica, their slot in the World Cup seemed all but assured.

Then the unthinkable happened: the United States lost to Mexico in the semifinals. Their eventual third place finish forced them into a two-game playoff against Italy. Whoever scored the most goals in those games would continue on to the World Cup. The loser would head home.

Team USA took the first game, played in Italy in late November, thanks to a clutch goal in the ninety-fourth minute by their youngest player, Alex Morgan. The second match was played on home turf in Illinois before a crowd of 9,500 spectators. Both teams were scoreless for most of the first half. Both wanted to head into the locker room with at least a one-goal advantage. But who, if anyone, would score?

Cue Megan Rapinoe. In the thirty-ninth minute, she collected a pass from Abby Wambach on the left side of the field. She dribbled toward the center. An Italian defender challenged her. Pinoe faked one way. The defender fell for it. Like a flash, Pinoe scooted past, darted toward the goal, and blasted off a kick. It looked good, but the Italian keeper slapped it away.

But not far enough. Amy Rodriguez raced in, nabbed the rebound right in front of the goal, and stabbed the ball into the net! Goal! When Italy couldn't answer, Team USA won the match and a trip to Germany in the summer of 2011 for the Women's World Cup.

Ahead of the World Cup, Pinoe decided to make a dramatic change that had nothing to do with her athletic training: She dyed her naturally brown hair platinum blond.

"Oh my gosh, what have you done?" her mother cried when she first saw her daughter's new do.

Denise might not have been a fan, but many soccer followers were. Pinoe's bold look made her instantly recognizable. It also matched her energetic, innovative style of play—the seemingly effortless way she maneuvered the ball with her feet, the stop-and-go running style that confounded defenders, the strength of her throw-ins, and the power of her kicks. After sitting out the 2007 Women's World Cup and the 2008 Olympics, she couldn't wait to bring that energy to the 2011 tournament.

She had to wait until late in the first match to do so. But since the team won 2–0 against North Korea, she tried not to be bothered by the fact that she'd only played eleven minutes. In the game against Colombia four days later, though, she got into the action at the start of the second half.

Correction: She *was* the action at the start of the second half!

Less than five minutes in, the ball bounced out of bounds off a Colombian player. Pinoe took the throw-in, then made a beeline for Colombia's penalty box. Teammate Lauren Cheney dished her the ball. Pinoe snared it just outside the circle and, without hesitation, turned and fired. The ball rocketed between two defenders. The keeper jumped, arms outstretched overhead. But she was a second too late. The ball flew just under the crossbar. Goal!

It was Pinoe's first World Cup goal. Her teammates swarmed her, but she had another celebration in mind. Jogging past the right corner, she grabbed a microphone from the field, dusted off its fluffy cover, and then put it to her mouth, belting out the opening lines of Bruce Springsteen's famous song "Born in the U.S.A."!

After the 3–0 win, she told reporters later that she and her teammates thought it would be funny to celebrate by serenading the audience. And she certainly felt like celebrating. "There's no better feeling for a footballer [soccer player] than scoring for their country in a competition like this. I'm absolutely thrilled."

She had reason to be thrilled later in the tournament, too. After a disappointing 2–1 loss to Sweden in the group stage, Team USA faced Brazil in the quarterfinals. Four years earlier, the Brazilians had beaten them in the semifinals—and then rubbed it in their noses by partying outside their rooms at the hotel where both teams were staying. Pinoe hadn't witnessed that scene, but she'd heard all about it from the players who had, including veteran star and future team captain Abby Wambach.

Thanks to Pinoe, Wambach would get her revenge. That quarterfinals match was a bizarre mixture of creative plays, missed chances, and heart-wrenching setbacks for both sides. In the second minute, Brazilian player Daiane scored an own goal that gave the United States a quick head start.

The score was still 1–0 when a US defender committed an egregious foul inside the penalty box and was expelled from the game. Brazil's star player, Marta, took the penalty kick, but keeper Hope Solo made the save.

Suddenly, though, the ref blew her whistle and

signaled for a redo of the kick. She believed Solo had come off the goal line before the kick, which was against the rules. This time, Marta's kick reached the back of the net.

USA 1, Brazil 1.

That's where the score stayed until the end of regulation time. Then two minutes into overtime, Marta blasted the ball past Solo.

Desperation set in on Team USA. If they didn't get a goal, they'd be done.

Scoreless minutes ticked by. Carli Lloyd belted a powerful blast that looked good—until it flew over the bar. More time passed, until there were just seconds remaining.

That's when Christie Rampone got the ball on their side of the field. She sent it to teammate Ali Krieger. Krieger passed it up to Lloyd. Lloyd took it over the half field line, looking for an opening, an open player, or anything or anyone that would give them the chance to score. Wambach was nearing the goal. But she was in traffic.

Then Lloyd spotted the player with the platinum blond hair off to her left. She sent her the ball.

Pinoe was still forty-five yards away from the goal. But her adrenaline was flowing, and time was running out. With a powerful swing, she booted a cross toward the goal.

The ball sailed high. Too high for the defenders to reach. Too high for the keeper to grab. But not too high for Abby Wambach. She skied above the others, and with the perfect touch—not too hard, not too soft—headed the ball just inside the right pole and into the net. Goal!

"I didn't see [Abby]," Pinoe later confessed, laughing, "but I knew she was going to be in there. She's always in there."

The crowd went crazy. "Oh, can you believe this?" the television announcer screamed. "Abby Wambach has saved the USA's life!" Wambach was swept up by her teammates on the sidelines. Pinoe raced in and jumped into her arms for a full body embrace, legs wrapped tight around her.

That goal was hailed as one of the most significant in women's soccer history and one of the best finishes to any game, period. And it wouldn't have happened if not for Megan Rapinoe. She wasn't done yet, either. With the score tied at 2–2, the match went to a penalty kick shootout. All five Team USA players scored, including Pinoe, who took the fourth shot. When Brazil made only three, the US team won.

Sadly, Team USA couldn't finish in equally dramatic fashion in the final match. After beating France 3–1 in the semifinals, they fell to Japan in a heartbreaking penalty kick shootout.

The mood on the plane ride home after that defeat was somber. But midway through the flight, Pinoe suddenly stopped thinking about the loss and started thinking about her future. Not just her role on the team, though that was part of it.

She was imagining a future in which she revealed a long-held secret to the world.

# CHAPTER 3
# 2012

## OUT AND PROUD

Pinoe was sitting across the aisle from her best friend and teammate, Lori Lindsey. The two were trying to keep each other's spirits up, when Lindsey paused, looked Megan in the eye, and said, "You know, you should really just come out. You need to come out."

By "come out," Lindsey didn't mean Megan should join her for dinner or go to a party. She was urging her friend to let the public know that she was gay.

Pinoe had known she was gay for years; though unlike many people who understand their sexual orientation at a young age, it hadn't really occurred to her until she was in college. "As soon as it clicked...I was like, 'Ah, she has arrived! She's here. Her life is beginning,'" she told a reporter a few years later.

Her sister Rachael already knew her secret.

Megan had told her back in college—right after Rachael revealed that she herself was gay. They'd told their family and closest friends, too, but chose to keep their private lives private.

But that choice troubled Pinoe. Hiding this important part of herself was exhausting. "The deeper in the closet you are," she once said, "the more it takes over your life."

With Lori Lindsey's words ringing in her ears, Pinoe decided on that plane ride to stop living the lie. She turned to her agent and told him she wanted to come out. "This is what I should do, what I want to do," she said. "What I need to do."

She wasn't doing it just for herself, but for anyone who struggled with their identity. She wanted to give them a voice, to show them that revealing who they truly were, while scary, was also incredibly freeing. She also hoped that by coming out, straight people who already knew her and who knew of her as a soccer player would realize that gay people were just that: people.

To reach as wide an audience as she could, Pinoe revealed her secret days before one of the biggest athletic competitions in the world: the 2012 Summer Olympics in London. "It's my job to say I'm gay," she told a reporter for *Out* magazine on July 2. "Which I am. For the record, I'm gay."

The public's response was immediate and, for the most part, wholly supportive. Pinoe herself felt freer than she ever had. And that freedom helped her play her best in the Olympics.

Taking the field in their bold red-and-white-striped jerseys, Team USA played its first match on July 25. France took an early 2–0 lead with goals at the twelve- and fourteen-minute marks. But the rest of the game belonged to the United States. They scored twice in the first half and twice in the second to win 4–2.

The United States overpowered Colombia in the early minutes of the next game, taking shot after shot on goal. But none of them went in.

In the thirty-third minute, Alex Morgan snared the ball in Colombia's half of the field. She sent it to Pinoe. Pinoe took a few quick dribbles, then caught the Colombians by surprise by blasting a shot from outside the box. Goal! Team USA put two more past the Colombian keeper, including a Rapinoe-to-Lloyd goal, to win 3–0.

They emerged victorious the next two games as well to reach the semifinals. There, they faced

Canada and its red-hot striker, Christine Sinclair. Sinclair had scored three goals already in the tournament. Against the United States, she added three more, with the first at twenty-two minutes in. Team USA couldn't answer that half. But they did soon after—and in spectacular, history-making style.

At the end of the fifty-third minute, Team USA was awarded a corner kick. Pinoe trotted to the left corner, placed the ball, and raised her arm to signal she was ready. She took a few quick steps, drew back her right foot, and kicked.

The ball soared high, curving toward the left post. Canada's defenders and keeper raced to stop it. There was a flurry of feet and legs, and then the ball dropped to the ground—just inside the goal line!

"I actually thought it was an own goal," Pinoe confessed.

Slow motion video confirmed what players on the field already knew. Pinoe had just made the first-ever Olimpico—as a goal scored directly from a corner kick is commonly known—in the history of the Olympics!

And she wasn't done yet. Three minutes after Sinclair scored her second goal to give Canada a 2–1 lead, Pinoe drilled the ball at the goal. It hit the post and then rolled over the line!

Sinclair erased that equalizer with yet another goal three minutes after that. But again, Team USA fought back and tied it up to send the match into overtime. When no one scored throughout the bulk of extra minutes, the game looked likely to be decided by a penalty kick shootout.

But it wasn't, thanks to a perfectly placed floating header from Alex Morgan in the final seconds. When the ball brushed beneath the crossbar and over the keeper's fingers, Team USA was in the finals!

Carli Lloyd was the star of the championship match, scoring both of the USWNT's goals in the 2–1 victory over Japan. The player who fed her an assist on the second, game-winning goal? Megan Rapinoe.

After the match, Pinoe had gracious words for Team USA's opponents. "They snatched our dream last year," she said, referring to the 2011 Women's World Cup, "and still we have that respect for that team." They showed that respect by foregoing their usual celebratory antics—cartwheels, front flips, and even a group rendition of the "worm"—and instead simply beamed and laughed when they took the stand to receive their gold medals.

"Sometimes I look at my medal in my sock drawer," Pinoe once said, "and I'm like, 'Wha–? Are you kidding me? This is so awesome!'"

Also awesome was the board of directors award she received a few months later from the Los Angeles Gay and Lesbian Center in recognition of her contribution to gay activism. Standing before a crowd of friends, family, fans, and supporters, Pinoe reflected on her own coming out journey in an impassioned, heartfelt speech.

"This is who I am," she said toward the end. "And I'm very proud of that."

# CHAPTER 4
# 2013–2017

## A VICTORY AND A KNEE

Pinoe's dynamic style of play, her historic Olimpico, and her openness about her sexuality catapulted her from soccer star to superstar after the 2012 Olympics. T-shirts bearing an outline of her famous bleached blond hair sold like crazy. Her social media sites blew up with followers all wanting to know more about her and, in many instances, to be *like* her. Megan accepted her newfound celebrity with bemused grace, but she didn't let the attention interfere with her next goal: winning the 2015 Women's World Cup.

She did make some changes in her life, however. After college and between stints with the USWNT, Pinoe had played on different teams in the Women's Professional Soccer (WPS) league and then, when the WPS folded in 2012, in US Soccer's short-lived W-League. In August 2013, she accepted an offer to play for Lyon of the Union of Europe Football

Association and moved to France. Living abroad was a fantastic experience, she said, and playing with high-caliber international stars improved her game.

She returned to the States in January 2014 to play for the Seattle Reign of the recently created National Women's Soccer League (NWSL). During the first home match on April 14, she suffered an injury to her left foot. She was sidelined for weeks. While that must have been frustrating, she gave herself time to heal so she'd be completely healthy for the CONCACAF qualifiers in October.

Luckily, her foot was back to 100 percent by that tournament. Under the guidance of the USWNT's new coach, Jill Ellis (Pinoe's former U-21 coach), and before home field crowds in Kansas City, Chicago, Philadelphia, and Washington, DC, Team USA won all three matches in the group stage. Pinoe helped that effort with the team's fifth and final goal in the second match, but it was Carli Lloyd and Abby Wambach who commanded the scoring that tournament, with Lloyd adding five and Wambach collecting seven, including four in the 6–0 victory against Costa Rica in the final game.

Then it was on to the 2015 Women's World Cup

in Canada. Thanks to Pinoe, the United States got a quick start in their first match against Australia. In the twelfth minute, she gathered a loose ball, whirled away to give herself space, and blasted a solid kick that deflected into the goal. Then, with the score 2–1 late in the second half, she ran with the ball down the entire length of the field to face the goalkeeper one-on-one. She fired off a kick, and just like that, the United States had their third goal.

The next match, against Sweden, pitted Team USA's current coach, Jill Ellis, against its previous coach, Pia Sundhage. That game, which Ellis compared to "two heavyweights going at it," ended in a scoreless draw. Nigeria was next. Wambach's lone goal was enough to give them the win and the top rank at the end of the group stage. Team USA beat Colombia 2–1 in the knockout round and China in the quarterfinals 1–0, and with a hard-fought 2–0 win over Germany in the semifinals, they reached their third consecutive World Cup finals.

And what a finals! First came Carli Lloyd's incredible sixteen-minute, three-goal performance—and Pinoe's gleeful shouts of "We're going to win the World Cup!" in the locker room at halftime. Japan pushed as hard as they could in the second half, but Team USA's momentum was just too powerful.

Final score: USA 5, Japan 2.

It was Team USA's third title, the most of any national team in the world. The weeks following that historic victory were a whirlwind of parades, television appearances, and even an October visit to the White House with then-president Barack Obama. Soon after that visit, Pinoe and her teammates traveled to Hawaii to train. And that's when it happened. On December 4, Pinoe tore the ACL in her right knee. It was a horrible blow for the soccer star. Having suffered the same injury twice in the other knee, she knew she'd be facing months of grueling rehabilitation. But she spun the news of her injury with her usual wit. "I'm currently accepting any recommendations for TV shows to binge watch and great restaurants that deliver in Seattle," she deadpanned.

She kept her fans updated on her progress with regular blog posts. Six months after her injury, she wrote about the importance of staying positive when rehabbing. "Speaking from experience," she wrote, "boy, will you be miserable if your focus lies in all the things you cannot do." Soon after that post, she added another that announced her return with this humorous yet touching opening line: "Welcome back to the Women's National Team (insert crying emoji face + big smile face)." And then, more than seven months after the ACL tear, she sent this jubilant message: "I did it. I am going to RIO!"

"RIO" was Rio de Janeiro, Brazil, and she was going there in August for the 2016 Summer Olympics. That she made the roster came as a surprise to many. Pinoe understood why—after all, she'd torn her ACL less than a year earlier and even though she was physically fit and mentally ready, she was thirty-one years old. There were others who were younger playing at a higher level than she was just then. But as Coach Ellis explained, "She is a game changer. And a game changer can come in for fifteen minutes and make a difference."

Unfortunately, Pinoe didn't get many opportunities to change the game. She sat out the first two matches (both wins), then started the third, only to come out after thirty-three minutes of play to make way for dynamic newcomer Mallory Pugh.

Three days later, Pinoe watched the first half of the quarterfinals with Sweden from the bench.

Team USA dominated the field but failed to put the ball in the goal. The Swedes didn't score, either, sending the teams to the locker room with a 0–0 tie. After the break, Sweden came on strong. With just their second shot on goal—*boom!* They powered one past keeper Hope Solo in the sixty-first minute.

Pinoe came into the game eleven minutes later. Shortly afterward, Alex Morgan picked up a botched clear right in front of Sweden's goal and drilled it into the net to make it USA 1, Sweden 1. That's how the score stayed through the rest of regulation time and thirty minutes of overtime. A penalty kick shootout followed. When it was over, Sweden had won, four penalty kicks to three.

Pinoe and her teammates were devastated. Never in the history of US women's soccer had they been bounced from the Olympics so soon. "The Olympics are definitely more awesome when you win Gold," she wrote on her blog.

Because of her knee, Pinoe hadn't made much of a splash in Rio. Back home in September, though, she and her knee grabbed headlines.

Since August, she had been following a growing controversy involving National Football League quarterback Colin Kaepernick. Kaepernick had started kneeling during the national anthem in protest of racial profiling faced by African Americans, police brutality, and racism in the United States. His protest was peaceful, but many people saw it as a sign of disrespect for the country and the flag.

Even though she had never experienced the same prejudice Kaepernick had, Pinoe believed in what he was doing. So, on September 4, she showed her support by taking a knee when the national anthem played before a Seattle Reign game. In doing so, she became the first white athlete, male or female, to publicly side with Kaepernick. "Being a gay American, I know what it means to look at the flag and not have it protect all your liberties," she told reporters. "It's the least I can do."

The blowback from her peaceful act was immediate, harsh, continuous, and sometimes even threatening. At one Reign game, she required a police escort to ensure her safety going to and from the field. But she kept kneeling. The statement she, Kaepernick, and others were sending was too important to her.

US Soccer, the governing body of the USWNT, felt pressure to discipline Pinoe for her actions. Instead, they issued a new bylaw stating that coaches and players must stand during the anthem. Pinoe respectfully complied—sort of. While she now stood, she refused to sing or put her hand over her heart.

That wasn't her only conflict with US Soccer in 2016. At the beginning of the year, she and teammates Carli Lloyd, Alex Morgan, and Becky Sauerbrunn filed a discrimination lawsuit against the organization. Players on the USWNT were paid less than their male counterparts on the US Men's National Team, they said in the lawsuit, despite having a much more successful history with three World Cup championships and four Olympic gold medals. By comparison, the men's team had won none.

While the lawsuit was being handled in court, Pinoe continued to speak out about racial injustice and inequality and advocate for human rights. Taking a stance wasn't always easy. Social media posts and spokespeople with conservative views made it clear they disagreed with her positions and her causes. "But it shouldn't be [easy]," she said. "This is what it's going to take for things to change, norms to change, conventions to change."

Pinoe knew change wouldn't happen overnight.

But she was more than willing to contribute her voice and her platform as an internationally renowned soccer player to her causes.

Pinoe also realized that if she was going to be back at the top of her game, she needed to make some changes in her own life. And those changes weren't going to be any easier to make.

# CHAPTER 5
# 2018–2019

## RED, WHITE, AND BLUE...AND PINK

Being benched at the 2016 Rio Olympics was a wake-up call for Pinoe. She knew her knee injury was only part of the reason she hadn't seen as much playing time. She was now thirty-one years old, and while she was still physically fit, she was starting to fall behind younger players. To stay competitive, she needed to make some changes, starting with how and what she ate. She found that she was often undereating or eating the right food at the wrong time. "I was not eating enough," she said, "which did not allow me to train as hard as I could have."

Pinoe knew just the person to help her make those changes: her life partner, Sue Bird. Bird, a point guard for the Seattle Storm of the Women's National Basketball Association (WNBA), was at the 2016 Rio Olympics competing with the US women's basketball team. When Pinoe met Bird, who is gay, she asked, "Why aren't we friends? We should be friends."

Their friendship turned into a relationship, and soon they were living together. And because Bird was into fitness and eating healthy, Pinoe started paying closer attention to her own nutrition habits. She changed her diet to include more vegetables and less sugar and junk. She focused on strengthening her body and increasing her flexibility, too. The changes made a world of difference to her performance on the field and made her "the strongest and fittest she's ever been," according to her sister Rachael.

Achieving a new level of fitness was vital for Pinoe. After sitting out much of the 2016 Olympics, she needed to show she could still be a valuable member of the USWNT.

Her campaign to regain her place as a starter began with a handful of games in 2017 and the first half of 2018. She played well, adding seven goals to bring her USWNT career total to thirty-eight by the end of July. But her ultimate goal for the year was to make a difference in the 2018 CONCACAF qualifiers in October.

Her wish was granted. Coach Ellis started her in the first match against Mexico. Pinoe was on fire right from the first minute. And in the third minute, she proved why she deserved the coach's trust.

Team USA got possession of the ball in their own half. They passed and dribbled it down field into Mexico's territory. Pinoe darted toward the goal, looking for a pass. It came but was deflected by a Mexican defender. Team USA regained control to the left of the box. Mexico's keeper, apparently suspecting a cross, charged out to challenge the ball handler, Lindsey Horan. In doing so, she left the goal wide open.

That's all Team USA needed. Horan sent a cross to Pinoe, who took two steps and booted it into the net without even breaking stride!

The United States pounded shot after shot at the keeper throughout the first half, all of them saved or misfired. Then finally Julie Ertz put one past the keeper to make it 2–0. Alex Morgan made it 3–0 with a header off a corner kick from Pinoe. Tobin Heath made it 4–0 with another header off a pass from Crystal Dunn. Another corner kick, this time by Heath, got lost in traffic in front of the goal. As the teams battled for the ball, Pinoe hovered outside like a cat waiting for a mouse to emerge from its hole. And when that "mouse" came, she pounced—and sent the ball right into the open net! A second goal from Morgan gave Team USA a final tally of 6 to Mexico's 0.

Pinoe and most of the starters rested on the sidelines during the next match, a 5–0 victory over Panama, but returned to the lineup for the third group stage game. It was another rout that saw multiple players scoring in the 7–0 win. Pinoe clocked her third goal of the tournament in the semifinals against Jamaica, another high-scoring match that ended 6–0 in Team USA's favor. The margin was closer in the finals against Canada, but in the end, the USWNT still emerged on top, 2–0.

Next stop: the 2019 Women's World Cup in France. But before that, there were practices and games.

And in January, there was a video interview.

It took place during a team photo shoot with *Eight by Eight*, a magazine dedicated to soccer. While Pinoe was preparing to have her picture taken, a reporter with a video camera asked her a simple question, referring to what would be an expected stop on the national team's victory tour: "Are you excited about going to the White House?"

In response, Megan snorted, rolled her eyes, and

said she wasn't going to the White House. She went on to say she was sure she wouldn't be invited. But if she was... "No," she repeated emphatically. "I'm not going to the White House."

A visit to the White House is a long-standing tradition for high-level championship teams from all sports. Pinoe and Team USA had gone in 2012 after winning the Olympic gold medal and again in 2015 after winning the World Cup. But a different president, Barack Obama, occupied the Oval Office then—a president Pinoe supported because she shared his values when it came to equality, racial justice, and human rights.

But there was a new president there now: Donald Trump. In Pinoe's opinion, Trump, his administration, and their agenda were morally wrong. So, no. She would not go to the White House.

*Eight by Eight* didn't release the video. Not right away, anyway.

Pinoe forgot about the video and focused on more important things, like staying healthy, keeping fit, eating right... and changing her hair.

"Pink?" Sue Bird was stunned when Pinoe told her that she planned to dye her signature bleached blond hair pink. Sue tried to talk her out of it by pointing out that if Team USA won the World Cup, photographers would swarm her to take her picture. Pinoe didn't really want to have pink hair for those photos, did she?

Pinoe did. The day before she boarded the plane for France, she dyed her hair pink. And just as her blond hair had done years earlier, her new look captivated her fans—and made her easy to pick out on the field!

Team USA's first match of the tournament was a 13–0 blowout against Thailand. Pinoe contributed one of those goals. But it was Alex Morgan's hot foot that made the difference; by the end of the game, she had booted in a total of five!

Coach Ellis sat several starters in the match against Chile to give the substitutes a chance to get over their jitters. "We need them to be in a good place," she said. And giving the starters a rest made sense, given that their third opponent was Sweden.

They won the games against Chile and Sweden 3–0 and 2–0, respectively, making it the only time in USWNT history that Team USA had blanked their group stage opponents during the World Cup. They also had the greatest number of goals ever scored in the group stage (eighteen).

The knockout match with Spain was a fierce battle almost from the start. In the seventh minute, Tobin Heath went on the attack, bringing the ball from the right side of the field into Spain's penalty box. She was about to kick when a Spanish player lashed out a leg and tripped her. The ref ruled it an egregious foul and awarded Team USA a penalty kick.

Pinoe took it. She approached the ball calmly and carefully, and then *boom!* She unleashed a drive right into the lower left corner! The goal was impressive. But what she did next was truly epic.

In 2011, Pinoe had delighted audiences by crooning Bruce Springsteen lyrics into a field microphone. This year, she took a quieter approach. After hurrying off the field, she faced the stands and struck a pose. Standing tall, arms outstretched, and with a serene smile on her face, she basked in the crowd's thunderous applause. She struck the same pose again after making the game-winning penalty kick in the seventy-fifth minute.

Pictures of that pose went viral almost overnight. So did something else: the video of Pinoe saying she wouldn't go to the White House. *Eight by Eight* had chosen to release the clip midway through the World Cup.

The next day, Pinoe held a press conference to address what she said in the interview. While she told reporters she stood by her comments, she did regret the possibility of the incident distracting her teammates.

"I was like 'Aaaargh!'" she said. "'Is this going to affect the team in some way?' I didn't want that to happen."

She needn't have worried. Her teammates, like Pinoe herself, were professional athletes used to the pressure of tense situations. On June 28, the day after her press conference, they headed onto the field for the quarterfinal match against France. Five minutes in, they were awarded a free kick. Pinoe took it—and converted it into a goal! She scored again in the second half to give Team USA a 2–0 lead. France closed the gap with a goal late in the game but couldn't add another. Final score: USA 2, France 1.

Team USA faced England in the semifinals four days later. They had one thing on their minds: winning.

Unfortunately, they took to the field without

Pinoe. She'd tweaked a hamstring muscle toward the end of the match with France and needed to rest it a few days. Her fans were relieved to know it wasn't something more serious but were disappointed not to see her and her pink hair tearing up and down the field.

But they weren't disappointed in Team USA or in Pinoe's replacement, Christen Press. In the tenth minute, Rose Lavelle dribbled the ball down into England's half. She threaded the ball between two defenders into open space to the right of the goal. Kelley O'Hara streaked in and collected it in the corner. She booted a cross. *Pow!* Press headed it into the goal!

England put in an equalizer nine minutes later. But Team USA was not to be denied. They pushed the ball into England's territory. Defenders pushed back. The ball bobbled loose. Lindsey Horan collected it and, with a well-placed kick, sent it sailing toward the goal. Alex Morgan raced in and headed it right into the goal.

England nearly tied it up in the eighty-fourth minute on a penalty kick. But US keeper Alyssa Naeher made an astonishing save, pouncing on the ball to preserve the lead.

Final score: USA 2, England 1.

The defending World Cup champions were going to their fourth World Cup finals! No way was Pinoe going to miss playing in that game. "I know this might be my last ride," she wrote in an online column two weeks earlier. "I really want one more World Cup trophy."

Two days after her thirty-fourth birthday, Pinoe took to the field with Team USA. Their opponent in the finals was the Netherlands. The United States hoped to continue their tournament streak of scoring in the first twelve minutes. But the Dutch fended off their attacks, and Team USA's scoring attempts missed their marks or were saved by the keeper. The Netherlands couldn't get on the board, either. The game was scoreless going into the half. When the game resumed, tension was running high. Who, if anyone, would score first?

Answer: Megan Rapinoe. In the sixty-first minute, the United States was awarded a penalty kick after Alex Morgan took a high kick to her shoulder. Megan had already put in two penalty kicks in the tournament. Fans and teammates hoped she could do it again.

She set the ball on the marker. Glanced over her

shoulder at the ref. Heard the whistle. She took a few quick steps forward and—*boom!*—unleashed a powerful kick. *Swish!*

Goal!

That penalty kick was Pinoe's sixth goal of the tournament, tying her with Alex Morgan for the most goals scored. It was also the fiftieth of her career. In making it, she became the oldest player in Women's World Cup history to score in a final, as well as the only player in a final to score off a penalty kick during regulation play.

The crowd was going crazy. And Megan gave them what they wanted. Trailed by her jubilant teammates, she ran to the left corner, stopped, spread her arms wide, and smiled.

Eight minutes later, it was Rose Lavelle who was smiling. Beaming, screaming, and laughing, actually. Because she had just dribbled the ball from the center line to the Dutch's penalty box, dodged between two defenders, and nailed a perfect shot into the goal!

The Dutch kept battling, but Team USA had momentum and energy on their side. Final score: USA 2, the Netherlands 0.

Minutes after that historic victory, the USWNT's

fourth overall, the players assembled on the field to receive their medals. Pinoe got even more hardware: the Golden Boot, for having scored the most goals in the least number of minutes played, and the Golden Ball, as the tournament's best player. Add in the World Cup trophy, and she didn't have enough hands to hold them all!

And the crowd's chant made the celebration even more memorable: "Equal pay! Equal pay!" The words in support of the team's quest for equal standing with the US Men's National Team were music to Pinoe's ears.

Pinoe reveled in the outpouring of admiration she and the team received when they returned home. She and her teammates took part in parades, gave speeches, and went on talk shows. Pinoe held one-on-one interviews with magazines, newspapers, and television news hosts, where she openly discussed her sexual orientation and her political views, as well as her storied soccer career. And on September 23, 2019, she accepted the Best FIFA Women's Player award, considered one of the top honors in women's international soccer.

But Pinoe never lost sight of herself and her values in the media and awards mayhem. A two-time

World Cup champion and an Olympian who fought her way through multiple injuries to regain her place at the top of the soccer world. An out and proud activist who didn't back down in the face of public backlash. A role model with pink hair and an impish smile whose personal motto is summed up in the two Arabic words tattooed on her wrist: "Trust yourself."

# MEGAN RAPINOE'S CAREER HIGHLIGHTS

## 2006

First US Women's National Team appearance,
July 23

First US Women's National Team goal,
October 1

## 2015

Played 100th cap, April 26

## 2011

FIFA Women's World Cup: Silver Medal

## 2012

London Olympics: Gold Medal

## 2015

FIFA Women's World Cup: Gold Medal

## 2016

Rio Olympics: Fifth Place

## 2019

FIFA Women's World Cup: Gold Medal
FIFA Women's World Cup Golden Ball
FIFA Women's World Cup Golden Boot
FIFA World Final Player of the Match
ESPY Award: Best Team